AF553726

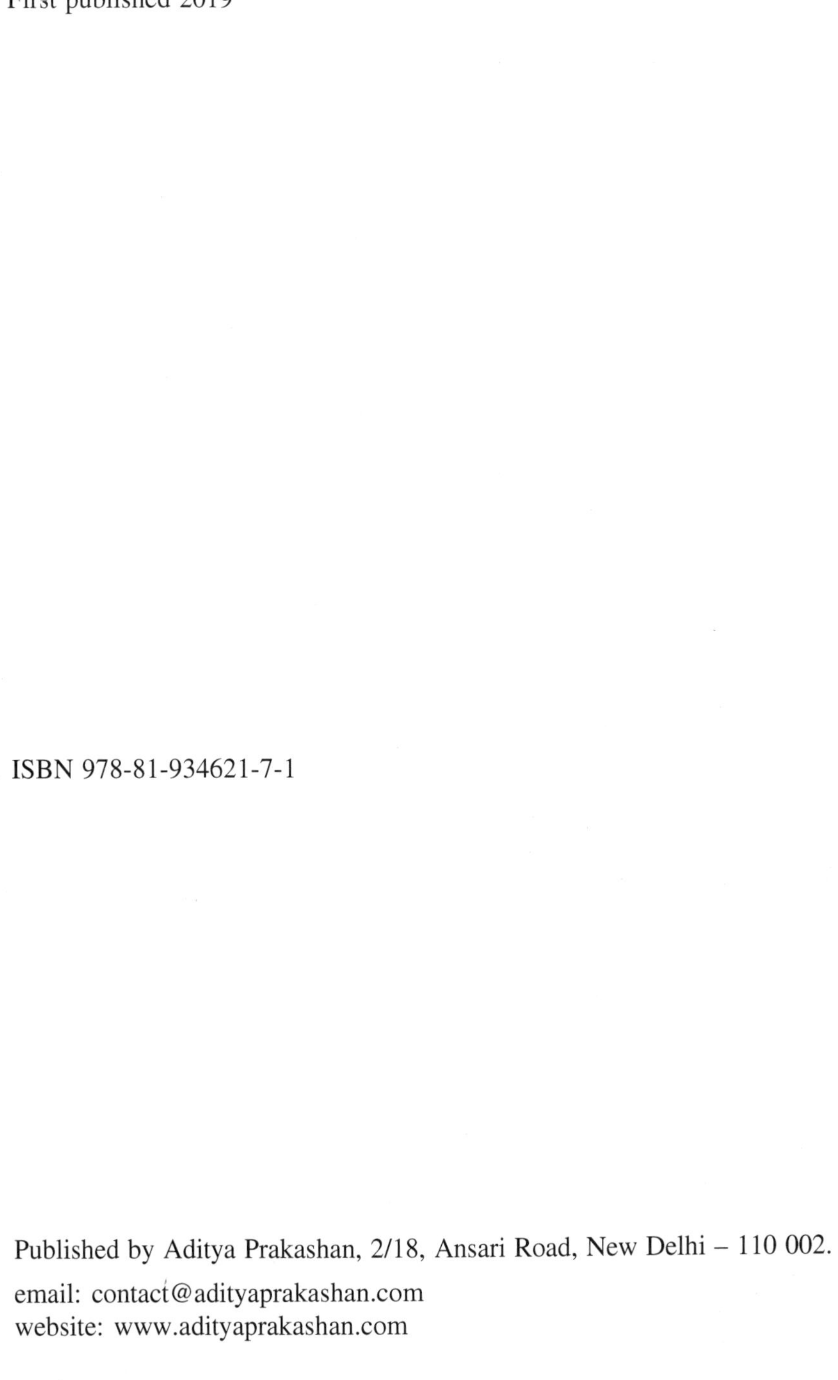

First published 2019

ISBN 978-81-934621-7-1

Published by Aditya Prakashan, 2/18, Ansari Road, New Delhi – 110 002.

email: contact@adityaprakashan.com
website: www.adityaprakashan.com

Printed at Replika Press Pvt. Ltd.

ESOTERIC BUDDHIST ASTROLOGY
Japanese *Sukuyōdō* and Indian Astrology

MICHIO YANO

English translation by *Bill M. Mak*

ADITYA PRAKASHAN
New Delhi

ESOTERIC BUDDHIST ASTROLOGY

Table of Contents

Preface to the English Translation

Over a quarter of a century has passed since the first edition of this book was published. After the third reprint was made in 1994, no more reprints were available from the publisher Tokyo Bijutsu. However, the demand for this work from readers appears to be great even today. A search on the internet showed that old copies of the work were sold at a very high price. Although I had always wanted to publish a second revised edition, my hectic schedule prevented me from doing so. When my friend Jun Yong Hoon published his Korean translation of my work, I was unfortunately unable to make any corrections or amendments. Recently, a project to translate the work into English was undertaken by Bill Mak, who is working at Kyoto University. Thus, I took this opportunity to make some corrections. Furthermore, thanks to an old manuscript of the *Xiuyao jing* purchased by the Science and Engineering Research Institute of Doshisha University, I have been involved since 2013 in a joint research project with Professor Takao Hayashi of the said institute on the *Xiuyao jing* as it was transmitted to Japan. From this research, I gained some new insights. In short, such opportunities led me to believe that it was time to publish a second, revised edition. Just at that moment, I was approached by Toyo Shoin who expressed interest in publishing a new edition of my book. The timing was excellent and I brought myself to the task right away.

In the third reprint of the first edition only a few apparent mistakes remained. Therefore, in this revised edition I have decided to adopt the same layout of the third reprint, make the necessary corrections and add some "additional notes" to the end of each chapter. In particular, I have included relevant references from a number of my Japanese works which were published afterward, namely, *The Astrologers' India* (*Senseijutsushi-tachi-no Indo*. Tokyo: Chūōkōronsha, 1992), *Japanese Translation of the Bṛhatsaṃhitā* (*Senjutsu daishūsei*. Tokyo: Heibonsha, 1995), *A History of Cultural Exchange in Astrology* (*Hoshiuranai-no bunka kōryūshi*. Tokyo: Keiso Shobo 2004), *Mathematical Way of Thinking in India—Historical Background of the IT powerhouse* (*Indo *sūgaku-no hassō: IT-taikoku-no genryū-wo tadoru*. Tokyo: NHK, 2011). An excerpt of Chapter Six, which was basically a report of my trip to India in 1985, together with some additional comments on Indian and Nepalese astrology which I observed in recent years are included in this English translation.

Moreover, in the second edition, I included two articles jointly written by myself and Takao Hayashi. The first one, titled "Two versions of the *Xiuyao jing* and the Doshisha Manuscript"『宿曜経』の二系統と同志社写本, was first presented at a conference of the Science and Engineering Research Institute of Doshisha University on 8 December, 2012. The paper was included in *The Science and Engineering Review of Doshisha University*, Vol.53, No.4 (January, 2013). The second one is titled "Notes on the Transmission of the *Sukuyōkyō*" 宿曜経伝承覚書, which was based largely on Hayashi's research.[1] These two articles are not included in this English translation.

Kyoto
January, 2018

Michio Yano

[1] A new study by Hayashi on one of the oldest manuscripts in Japan is forthcoming: "Sukuyōkyō shahon oboegaki: Shinpukuji shahon-to koissaikyō shahon" 宿曜経写本覚書—真福寺写本と古一切経写本.

Preface

The purpose of this book is not to give a full exposition on Esoteric Buddhist astrology or the Japanese Sukuyōdō school of astrology. Neither is it an attempt to clarify the origin or details of Indian astrology. Rather, this book is an attempt to demonstrate the important role astrology has played, as a facet of the ancient world, in the history of contacts among civilizations across space and time.

What has interested me the most is the history of cultural exchange in the field of ancient astronomy of which astrology is a part. Otto Neugebauer in his *The Exact Sciences in Antiquity* had vividly described the dissemination of mathematical astronomy among the ancient civilizations. Focusing in particular on Mesopotamia, Neugebauer had shown brilliantly how Mesopotamian astronomy spread to the Mediterranean world and India. I was initially trained in classical Sanskrit philology. One of my fields of research is the application of Neugebauer's methodology to India. In particular, recently I have been working on the transmission of Indian sciences to the Islamic world.

Astrology has often been described as a "pseudo-science" in the present day and is not considered a subject of serious academic inquiry. Nonetheless, it should be borne in mind that until the advent of modern science, astrology and astronomy had been inseparable from each other. In contrast to astronomy, which addresses the regularity of celestial phenomena by mathematical means, astrology is concerned with the relationship between celestial phenomena and human behaviors, in response to the primordial human desire to know the future. Astrology was an attempt to bring together the knowledge of the heavens and that of the earth by turning the sacred knowledge of the heavens into mundane knowledge. It is thus of no surprise that astrology was ultimately supported by the wider, general society in contrast to astronomy whose true mastery remains only in the hands of the specialists.

The present work deals with the transmission of astrology, not astronomy, from India to Japan. Since many elements of what is called

Indian astrology originated in the West, it is inevitable to touch on the latter. In 1981, when I was lecturing at the Faculty of Letters of Kyoto University, I had an opportunity to read a Chinese astrological text called *Xiuyao jing* 宿曜經 at the students' request. As our knowledge on the text as well as on other related materials grew, this interesting "sūtra" became comprehensible to me and I was prompted to publish the work. In 1985, as a part of a research project funded by a grant from the Japanese government, I published a report titled "The relationship between *Xiuyao jing* and Indian astrology/astronomy." The present book is an expanded version of this work, together with modifications catering to a more general audience.

Previous research on the *Xiuyao jing* was made by Morita Ryūsen 森田龍僊, author of *Mikkyō Senseihō* 密教占星法 (Two volumes, Kōyasan, 1941. Reprinted, Kyoto: Rinsen Shoten, 1974). An erudite monk from Kōyasan, Morita came from the living tradition of esoteric astrology and his work was the fruit of years of study of the voluminous Buddhist canon. With today's knowledge, however, we can no longer accept Morita's work without reservation; the book is nonetheless a mine of information and insight when read in a critical way. Though not as well-versed in the Buddhist texts as Morita was, I tried to treat esoteric Buddhist astrology in its historical context more objectively, and more broadly than Morita.

I would like to take this opportunity to thank especially Ms. Aoki Yaemi and Ms. Shimizu Junko who attended my lectures at Kyoto University with great enthusiasm and had raised many thought-provoking questions. Some of the questions left unanswered then are dealt with here in this book. Nevertheless, not all questions have been resolved and without a doubt there also remain some errors. Feedback from readers would therefore be greatly appreciated.

I am greatly indebted to my teacher, Professor David Pingree of Brown University, for introducing me to the study of Indian astronomy and astrology. I have written several papers in English and discussed some of the topics in this book as a token of appreciation to him. I wanted to show that the transmission of astrology from the Hellenistic world to India, which was clearly demonstrated by Professor Pingree, reached as far as Japan.

As for the relationship between Chinese astronomy/astrology and their Indian counterparts, the works of Prof. Yabuuti Kiyosi 藪内清 must not go unmentioned. I had the great fortune to attend his class, thanks to our common interest in Indian astronomy. I would like to make this book a dedication to my guru who turns eighty years old this year.

April, 1986 Michio Yano

Translator's Note

This English translation was initially based on the 1986 edition of *Mikkyō senseijutsu* and was subsequently revised with the 2013 revised Japanese edition. Changes from the Japanese edition (2013) include the addition of an expanded bibliography and some minor revisions made by the author himself. Sanskrit, Chinese and Japanese technical terms follow largely the academic convention for the respective languages. In some cases, analogous ideas and concepts such as the lunar mansions are rendered into forms which the context demands (*nakṣatra* in Sanskrit, *xiu* 宿 or "[lunar] lodge" in Chinese, or simply "mansion" when ambiguous). Footnotes are provided by the author unless otherwise indicated ("trans. note"). Some of the original photos have been replaced due to copyright reasons or the availability of photos of better quality. Romanization of Chinese characters follows the Pinyin or the Hepburn system depending on the context which calls for Chinese or Japanese reading respectively.

The translation was completed after Prof. Michio Yano had gone through numerous drafts since the summer of 2013. Thanks go to Prof. Johannes Bronkhorst, Dr. Kiyokazu Okita and Rolf Giebel for their advices on various aspects of the translation, to Masahiro Ueda for his editorial assistance, and to Elizabeth Tinsley and Jeffrey Kotyk, and especially Dr. Kristina Buhrman and Dr. Michelle McCoy, for proofreading the entire translation.

Kyoto, January 2018 Bill M. Mak

I. INTRODUCTION

1. *Xiuyao jing*: A Sūtra Proclaimed by the Bodhisattva Mañjuśrī

In Japanese, the *Xiuyao jing* is usually pronounced *Sukuyōkyō* and the astrological school that was developed based on the teachings of this text reads as Sukuyōdō 宿曜道, or "School of the *Nakṣatra*-s and Luminaries."[2] To most Japanese, *xiu* 宿 may be pronounced indiscriminately as either *suku* or *shuku*, and thus one finds in fact entries for both *sukuyō* and *shukuyō* in the Kōjien 広辞苑 dictionary. The "experts," however, recognize the reading *suku* as the professional one, and thus distinguish themselves from the amateurs in this particular way. Incidentally, the library card system from the Kyoto University Library has adopted the *shuku* reading.

As a sūtra, the *Xiuyao jing* is considered a Buddhist scripture, included in the Chinese Buddhist Canon. The text is found in Volume Twenty-One (esoteric section) of the *Taishō Tripiṭaka* compiled during the Taishō Era (1912–1926), where it carries the rather verbose title *Sūtra on Auspicious and Inauspicious Times and Days, Good and Bad Nakṣatra-s and Luminaries Proclaimed by the Bodhisattva Mañjuśrī and the Sages* (*Wenshushili pusa ji zhuxian suoshuo jixiong shiri shan'e xiuyao jing* 文殊師利菩薩及諸仙所說吉凶時日善惡宿曜經). While it is customary for Buddhist texts to begin with the phrase "Thus I have heard" (Ch. *rushi wo wen* 如是我聞; Skt. *evaṃ mayā śrutam*) to indicate the authenticity of the text as the Buddha's words, the *Xiuyao jing*, as the title itself suggests, was ascribed to "the bodhisattva Mañjuśrī and sages."

The Sanskrit name of the bodhisattva Mañjuśrī was translated as Wenshu shili 文殊師利 in Chinese, commonly abbreviated as Wenshu (Jp. Monju). In Japanese, there is an idiom, "Where three persons gather, there is the wisdom of Monju." Indeed, among the numerous Bodhisattvas, Mañjuśrī is known for his wisdom. According to the title,

---

[2] Translator's note: In this book, *xiu* 宿 and *yao* 曜, as appear in the title *Xiuyao jing* 宿曜経, are translated as "*nakṣatra*" and "luminary," which refer to the lunar mansions and the planets (including the Sun and Moon) respectively.

this *sūtra* is a treatise proclaimed by the Bodhisattva and the sages concerning auspicious and inauspicious times and days, good and bad *nakṣatra*-s and luminaries. The meaning of the title will become clear as we examine the contents.

Regarding its authorship, "Mañjuśrī and the sages" may not have been the authors of the sūtra at all: the attribution of a work to the legendary Bodhisattva Mañjuśrī may just be an appeal to authority. Moreover, it remains doubtful whether the *Xiuyao jing* was actually translated from a Sanskrit original.

Fig.1 Star Maṇḍala 星曼荼羅

From outer ring: 28 nakṣatra-s, 12 zodiacal signs, 7 stars of Ursa Major (Big Dipper) and 9 luminaries. In the middle is the golden cakra of Śākyamuni on top of Mount Meru. Collection of Hōryūji 法隆寺.

According to the introductory statement at the beginning of the *Xiuyao jing*, the text was produced by a team of three: it was first orally taught by Amoghavajra (Ch.Bukong, Jp.Fukū 不空), then transcribed by Shi Yao 史瑶, and finally revised by Yang Jingfeng 楊景風. Among the three, Amoghavajra was a monk of Indian origin while Shi Yao and Yang Jingfeng were Chinese. While their exact roles in the production of the text will be discussed later, for the moment we should say that the *Xiuyao jing* came into existence by 764 CE and that Amoghavajra was responsible for its composition.

The content of the *Xiuyao jing* pertains exclusively to Indian astrology and is completely unrelated to Buddhist teachings. However, in the guise of a Buddhist text, this work was given a new life and was disseminated to Japan, leading to the establishment of a Japanese school of astrology—Sukuyōdō.

When Kūkai 空海, also known posthumously as Kōbō Daishi 弘法大師, traveled to China and received the teachings of Esoteric Buddhism, forty years had passed since the *Xiuyao jing* appeared. Huiguo 惠果, the teacher of Kūkai, was the direct disciple of Amoghavajra. Thus, through this lineage from Amoghavajra the Indian, through Huiguo the Chinese, to Kūkai the Japanese, the Esoteric school known as Shingon was established and eventually blossomed in Japan. In 806 CE, Kūkai brought a great number of Buddhist sūtras back to Japan. According to the *Gōshōrai mokuroku* 御請來目録 (Catalogue of texts brought from China), out of the one hundred and forty-two newly translated texts, one hundred and eighteen of them—that is, over eighty percent—were translated by "Amoghavajra the Tripiṭaka Master."

The title of our text is included also in this list, together with two additional pieces of information: "two fascicles" and "forty folios." A text of the same title was brought to Japan again in 847 CE by the Tendai master Ennin 円仁 (794–864 CE) and in 858 CE by Enchin 円珍 (814–91 CE). The Sukuyōdō school of astrology was formed shortly after this, inspired by the text, and by the mid-Heian period its popularity rivaled that of the mainstream Onmyōdō 陰陽道, "the School of Ying and Yang". In *The Tale of Genji* (*Genji Monogatari* 源氏物語), some professional astrologers are referred to as "people wise in the teachings of the Sukuyō."[3]

[3] There have been attempts to unravel the structure of *The Tale of Genji* from the viewpoint of esoteric Buddhist astrology (Ōkubo 1981).

In this book, I wish to show how the *Xiuyao jing* came into being and to what extent it reflects Indian astrology. Furthermore, I shall describe the relationship between this work and other works of esoteric Buddhist astrology.

Fig.2 Mañjuśrī on Lion, China, Tangut State of Xixia, Khara-khoto. 12th–13th century. 96×60cm. Roll on silk. Inv. no.HH–2447.

(Photograph © The State Hermitage Museum. Photo by Leonard Kheifets.)

2. Indian Astrology According to Amoghavajra

Kakushō Edition of the *Xiuyao jing*

The *Xiuyao jing* in the *Taishō Tripiṭaka* is an edition based on the *Korean Tripiṭaka*, collated with variant readings from the Ming edition, as indicated in the apparatus. While there are minor differences between the Korean and the Ming editions, the two are roughly the same. As such, we may safely call this version of the *Xiuyao jing* included in various Chinese Tripiṭakas the "Continental edition."

Older Japanese manuscripts of the *Xiuyao jing*, however, provide readings that vary from those of the Continental edition. When the learned monk Kakushō 覚勝 published his edition of the *Xiuyao jing* in 1736, he included a critical apparatus with variant readings from a number of Japanese manuscripts, in addition to those of the Korean and Ming editions. In 1981, I made a comparison of the Kakushō edition from the Kyoto University collection with the Continental edition. The superiority of the Kakushō edition became evident to me. I recently had the opportunity to examine a few manuscripts from the collections of Tōji Temple in Kyoto and the Kōyasan University Library. I could confirm that the Kakushō edition had faithfully preserved the Japanese manuscript tradition of the *Xiuyao jing*. Although the manuscripts and Kakushō's edition were preserved here in Japan, they were either not known or ignored by the editors of the Taishō Tripiṭaka. There are a number of other esoteric astrological texts besides the *Xiuyao jing* that were similarly given little attention by the compilers of the Taishō Tripiṭaka at that time. In the present work, I have supplied new insights gleaned from the Kakushō edition.

One shortcoming of the Kakushō edition that I must point out, however, is the difficulty in distinguishing between the original text and the commentary. The text proper and the commentary by Yang Jingfeng were written in characters of the same size and thus ran together;[4]

[4] Translator's note: Interlinear notes known as *jiazhu* 夾註 (Jp. *warichū* 割注) are usually written or printed in smaller font.

moreover, the phrase "according to Jingfeng" is sometimes missing. Nonetheless, as we shall see, the Kakushō edition is in fact closer to the original text than the Continental edition. From this point on, we shall call the Kakushō edition and the manuscripts it was based on the "Japanese edition."

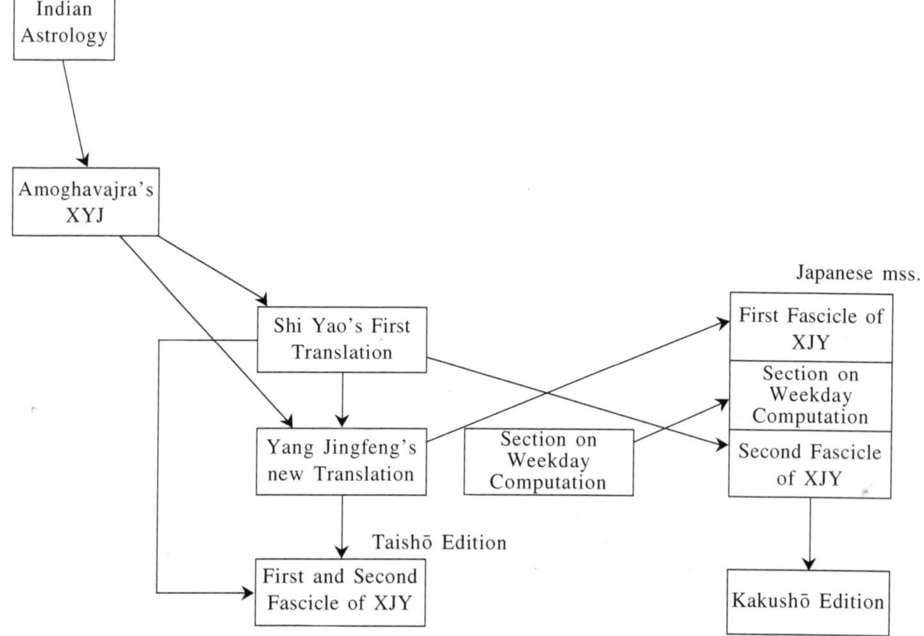

Fig.3 The Transmission of the *Xiuyao jing*.

The Sinicization of Indian Astrology

The *Xiuyao jing* consists of two fascicles. The first fascicle begins with the following introduction:

> This text was translated by the venerable Master in the second year of Qianyuan 乾元 [759 CE]. It was written down and edited by Shi Yao, the magistrate (*sima* 司馬) of Duanzhou 端州. The sections were not arranged in an orderly fashion and the content was confusing, making it difficult for the learners to make use of. The lay disciple Yang Jingfeng, following the intimate instruction of the Master, carefully copied the text with corrections and annotations and completed a draft of it. All the members of our school now have a copy of it, [written in] the spring of the year Jiachen 甲辰, second year of Guangde 廣德 of the Tang Period.

In the Japanese edition, this passage is followed by an interesting remark:

> There are two editions of the text. One is the edition initially written down by Shi Yao. The other is the edition emended and annotated by Yang Jingfeng.

In other words, according to this remark, the two fascicles of the *Xiuyao jing* represent in fact the first translation by Shi Yao, who composed the text initially, and the amended edition that came from the hand of Yang Jingfeng. This additional remark is not found in the Continental edition and was possibly inserted by a Japanese scribe. Nonetheless, since it is found in both the Kōyasan Kongō Sanmai-in 高野山金剛三昧院 manuscripts and the Tōji 東寺 manuscript, the remark must be very old.[5] With this in mind, upon actual comparison of the two fascicles, the following conclusion becomes evident.

To put it simply, the second fascicle of the *Xiuyao jing* should be the first translation by Shi Yao, who put the text into writing in 759 CE, while the first fascicle is in fact the emended version completed by Yang Jingfeng in 764 CE. We may ask then why the first translation was not discarded after the new version was completed, and why the two texts were joined together while being treated as individual fascicles. To answer these questions, we must examine Amoghavajra's role as the "translator" of the text.

As briefly mentioned before, the *Xiuyao jing* is attributed to the Bodhisattva Mañjuśrī and sages. However, a number of elements of Indian astrology described in the work have in fact a Hellenistic origin. These are ideas that were imported into India at around the second or third centuries CE, before they were transmitted to China. Such elements were in their primitive forms in view of the development of Indian astrology, as specific techniques are not mentioned. Thus, in my opinion, the *Xiuyao jing* is not a translation from a particular Indic text, but rather a compendium of Indian astrological knowledge as known to Amoghavajra himself. As a fervent preacher of the Mañjuśrī cult in China, it is only natural that Amoghavajra attributed this newly composed work to the Bodhisattva.

The formation of the *Xiuyao jing* is thus as follows. First, Amoghavajra taught the text orally to a certain audience based on his

---

[5] The two manuscripts are from the twelfth century and the Kamakura Period respectively. Translator's note: For a description of the manuscripts, including their date and other details from the colophons, see Yano and Hayashi 2013, Yano 2016, and Hayashi (forthcoming).

knowledge of Indian astrology. At that time, the language would have been partly Sanskrit and partly Chinese. His disciple Shi Yao wrote down what he heard in Chinese. The terms transliterated from Sanskrit, however, appear awkward. Moreover, Amoghavajra's oral teaching might not have been coherent to begin with. Five years later, Amoghavajra asked his lay disciple Yang Jingfeng to revise the work. Compared to Shi, Yang appeared to demonstrate a greater command of the literary Chinese language and completely revamped the first translation following the direction of Amoghavajra. Firstly, he changed the order of the contents and subdivided the work into six chapters (*pin* 品) under different headings. Then, he revised the awkward wordings of the first translation and rendered the text more comprehensible to the Chinese readers. Furthermore, he supplied his own annotations to the work. Finally, Yang supplemented the work with an extra "section" (*zhang* 章) entitled "Weekday Computation" (Suanyaozhi zhang 算曜直章) at the end. As Yang noted in the commentary included in the text, the fact that this additional part was labeled "section" (*zhang*) and not "chapter" (*pin*) suggests that it is not to be attributed to the Bodhisattva Mañjusrī. While the content of this "section" will be examined in detail later, it is of interest to note that it is not found in the Continental edition and was transmitted only in the Japanese edition. In the Continental edition, however, in a comment found at the beginning of the fourth chapter, Yang himself referred to this section appended to the end of the work. We could therefore say that this section must have appeared in the original text and was somehow lost during its transmission in China, as shown in the Korean and Ming editions.

It has become evident to me that the two-fascicled *Xiuyao jing* in fact consists of two translations of the same text whose order was reversed. However, no other modern researchers seem to have noticed this. This may be due to the notable differences between the two fascicles in terms of their content. On this point, Morita wrote, "Although it has been recognized as fact that Shi Yao's edition came out first, I think it was lost after the Jingfeng edition [had come out]."[6]

Morita mentioned in his work that during the Edo Period there was a theory that the first and second fascicles comprised two distinct editions by Yang Jingfeng and Shi Yao respectively, but discarded the view as a "strange idea."

---

[6] Morita 1941:94.

The transmission through the lineage Amoghavajra-Shi-Yang entailed a sinicization process of Indian astrology. While Shi's translation was somewhat jumbled, it has an Indian flavor not found in Yang's. On the other hand, while Yang's translation must have been more comprehensible for the Chinese readers, some interesting details from the Indian perspective were taken away. As a result, the old translation was not abandoned despite the appearance of a new one.

If one examines the titles in the Japanese manuscripts, one may see the difference between the two fascicles. In the Continental edition, the title of the second fascicle mentioned at the very beginning of the text is identical to that of the first fascicle. The first fascicle of the Japanese manuscript, on the other hand, has a shorter title, namely, *Sūtra on the Nakṣatra-s and Luminaries as Proclaimed by the Bodhisattva Mañjuśrī* 文殊師利菩薩所說宿曜經 "and the sages" 及諸仙, "auspicious and inauspicious time and day" 吉凶時日, and "good and bad" 善惡 are missing from the title. If the two fascicles were supposed to be joined together as one text, they should have the same title. In fact, the Continental edition has just that.

Amoghavajra: The Author

As explained before, it would be better to describe Amoghavajra as the author, rather than translator, of the *Xiuyao jing*. Now, let us examine the life of Amoghavajra according to the *Song Biographies of Eminent Monks* (*Song gaoseng zhuan* 宋高僧傳). (Figs.4&5 are on page 12).

The name Amoghavajra in Sanskrit was translated as Bukong Jingang 不空金剛 in Chinese, abbreviated as Bukong, or else translated phonetically as Amuqubazheluo 阿目佉跋折羅. Born in North India to a Brahmin family, Amoghavajra lost both his parents at a young age. At the age of fifteen, while accompanying his uncle on a journey to China, he became by chance a disciple of Vajrabodhi, an Indian monk preaching Esoteric Buddhism in China at that time. Having quickly acquired the knowledge of his teacher, Amoghavajra wished to travel across India in search of Buddhist texts. In 741 CE, his teacher passed away. Following the advice of his late teacher, Amoghavajra set off to India and Ceylon in the twelfth month of the same year. Five years later, after having collected numerous esoteric texts from both places, he returned to China. Amoghavajra served three consecutive Tang rulers: Emperor Xuanzong 玄宗, Emperor Suzong 肅宗, and Emperor Daizong 代宗, making prognostications and performing placatory and prosperity

Fig. 4 Kūkai.
(https://upload.wikimedia.org/wikipedia/commons/9/98/Kobo_Daishi_ %28Taisanji_Matsuyama%29.jpg)

Fig.5 Amoghavajra.
(https://upload.wikimedia.org/wikipedia/commons/b/b6/Portrait_of_Amoghavajra%2C_14_century%2C_National_Museum%2C_Tokyo.jpg)

rituals. With his unusual talents, Amoghavajra was responsible for turning Mantrayāna or Esoteric Buddhism into the state religion of China at that time. Among his many disciples, Huiguo 惠果 chiefly continued the lineage. On the fifteenth day of the sixth month of the ninth year of *Dali* 大暦 (774 CE), Amoghavajra passed away at the age of seventy. It was said that Emperor Daizong held a grand funeral for the Master that lasted three whole days.

In the *Song Biographies of Eminent Monks*, Amoghavajra's supernatural abilities to halt rainstorms and invoke rain in the time of drought are described in detail. Such acts without a doubt contributed to the promotion of Esoteric Buddhism as the state religion. There are also numerous similar legends of Kūkai in Japan. Kūkai himself seemed to be aware of the fact that the year of his birth coincided with the year Amoghavajra passed away. This is one of the bases of the legend that Kūkai was himself a reincarnation of Amoghavajra.

In the first year of Yongtai 永泰 (765 CE), the year following the translation of Amoghavajra's *Xiuyao jing* "proclaimed by the bodhisattva Mañjuśrī," Amoghavajra was promoted to the official position of "Specially Advanced Probationary Chief Minister of the Court of State Ceremonial" 特進試鴻臚卿 and was conferred the title "Tripiṭaka Master, Great Revealer of Wisdom" 大廣智三藏 by Emperor Daizong. Forty years later, Kūkai brought Amoghavajra's *Xiuyao jing* with him to Japan, with the expectation that the text would play an important role in protecting the state.

Chapter One—Additional Notes

In November 2011 the Science and Engineering Research Institute of Doshisha University made a successful bid for a manuscript of the *Xiuyao jing* auctioned at an antiquarian exhibition held at the Tokyo Antiquarian Book Hall. The manuscript was dated 1322 CE. To evaluate the value of the manuscript, it was necessary to compare it with the oldest extant manuscript of the *Xiuyao jing*, now kept in the Reihōkan 霊宝館 of Kōyasan. The Kōyasan manuscript was particularly precious to me as I did not have the opportunity to examine it when I visited Kōyasan in 1985. Subsequently, color photos of the manuscripts were made available to me. This collection contains two manuscripts, both kept in container no.25 of the Hōjuin collection. The label "Collection of Hōjuin" was placed on the two manuscripts apparently at a later date, while "Collection of Muryōjuin" was clearly written on the front and inner covers of both manuscripts. The first manuscript, no.124, contains both first and second fascicles in one volume with sixty-three folios in total. The second manuscript, no.125, contains also the first and second fascicles but are separated into two volumes. According to Yamamoto Chikyō,[7] the first manuscript is dated 1160 CE, while the second manuscript is dated from the "Heian Period," which would make it likely the oldest manuscript extant. The Doshisha University manuscript can be said to be of a somewhat later period, but it is still extremely valuable as it comes from the lineage of the old manuscripts brought to Japan by Kūkai. The manuscript may be accessed and downloaded from the "Doshisha University Academic Repository."[8]

For details on the manuscript tradition, see Yano & Hayashi (2012), Appendices I and II in the second Japanese edition.

[7] "Hōjuin-no zōsho," *Mikkyō gakkaihō*, 1975.

[8] https://doors.doshisha.ac.jp/opac/opac_link/bibid/BB12284151/?lang=1

II. SOURCES AND EVOLUTION OF *XIUYAO JING*

1. Indian Astral Science

Before describing how the components of the *Xiuyao jing* correspond to various elements of Indian astral science, let us clarify a few points concerning the nature of the Indian astral texts that predated the *Xiuyao jing*. While it might be difficult to periodize the history of Indian astral science with absolute certainty, one may make a broad classification according to its main content:

i) Indigenous Indian elements prior to Hellenism
ii) Western elements after Hellenism
iii) Islamic elements

Among these three, Islamic elements will not be touched upon here since their first appearance in Indian literature was much later than the *Xiuyao jing*. On the other hand, Greek astral science, developed at the peak of Hellenism, spread to India in around the second and third century CE and was later skillfully nativized. These Hellenistic elements have coexisted with the older Indian astral science up to the present day. In fact, much of what is now known popularly as "Indian astrology" has a Hellenistic origin.

Cultural exchange between India and the West may be traced far back in history. There have been contacts between the two cultures in northwestern India since the establishment of Greek colonies in Bactria in the third century BCE. Among the best-known instances of the East-West intellectual exchange during that period is a work known as *Milindapañha*, or *Milinda's Questions*, which describes the Greek king Menander's queries to the Buddhist monk Nāgasena concerning the essence of Buddhism and the latter's response. However, at that time the astral science was not yet fully developed in Greece. In fact, mathematical astronomy was not advanced enough to make horoscopy possible, that is, as a specialized form of astral science.

Around the mid-second century BCE, Babylonian functional astronomy and Greek geometrical astronomy merged in the hands of

Hipparchus of the Mediterranean island of Rhodes to form what was to become the foundation of astral science in the ancient world. At that time, astrology was also at a turning point and horoscopy was growing in popularity. A horoscope-like object giving the planetary positions dated to April 29, 410 BCE, has been discovered in what was then Babylonia. The earliest horoscope discovered so far in the Greek world is dated July 7, 62 BCE From that time up until Ptolemy's *Tetrabiblos* in the mid-second century CE, Greek astrology underwent rapid development.

Just at that time the trade winds spanning the Indian Ocean were discovered and trade between the Mediterranean and the west coast of India began to thrive. As we enter the Roman Age, Alexandria, located at the mouth of the Nile River with a long tradition of Greek science, became the center from which Hellenistic culture was exported to all the neighboring regions. In this way, Greek astronomy and astrology began to spread to India around the second century CE. In the Indian astral works of subsequent eras one may find many instances of computational techniques and loanwords borrowed from Greek astronomy. While it has been noted in the past that many such special terms in Indian astronomy have a Western origin, until recently no text was known as concrete evidence demonstrating how the Greek astral science was introduced to India. The *Yavanajātaka* is such a text. An edition of this work was published by Pingree in 1978.

The *Yavanajātaka* was known in the past through fragmentary excerpts cited in various Indian astrological texts. The full manuscript was discovered only later in Nepal. The title *Yavanajātaka* in Sanskrit means "Genethliacal Astrology of the Greeks" (the word *jātaka* is unrelated to the Buddhist literary genre of the same name, see p.114, fn.67). It is based on a Sanskrit prose "translation" from Greek dated around 150 CE by the Greek King Yavaneśvara, which was then versified by Sphujidhvaja in 269 CE.[9] I put "translation" in quotation marks because, as with the case of the *Xiuyao jing*, the existence of a Greek original cannot be ascertained and, moreover, the contents of the extant *Yavanajātaka* have been thoroughly Indianized or Sanskritized. Nevertheless, it is clear to any reader of this work that the bulk of its content has a Hellenistic origin.

The *Yavanajātaka* was the starting point of Indianized Greek/ Babylonian astrology. The year 150 CE, when this text was first

[9] Translator's note: See comments at the end of the chapter.

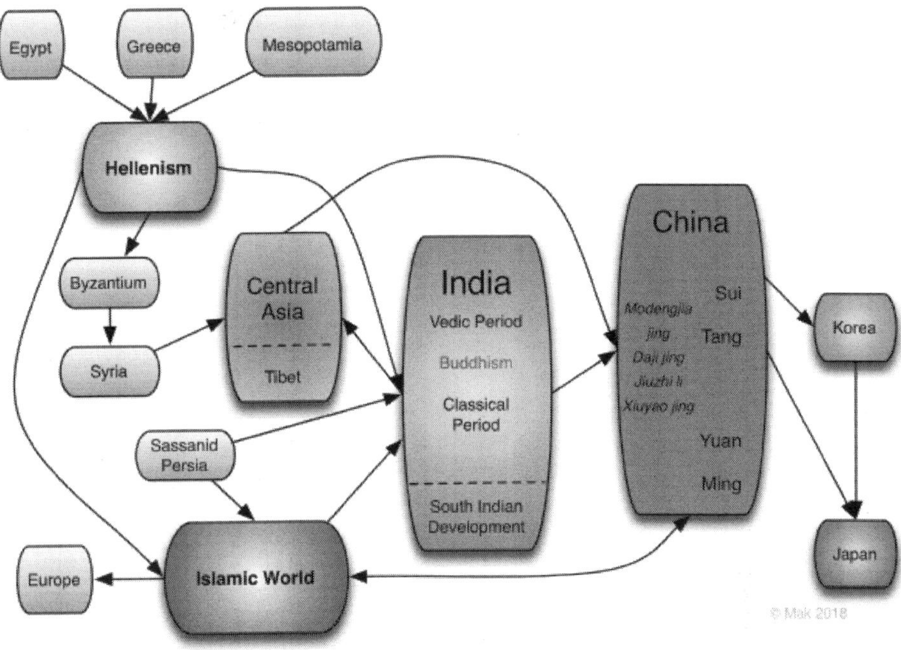

Fig.6 Transmission of Genethliacal astrology.

Fig.7 Horoscopic representation at the coronation of Antichos I of Commagene.
(© B.L. van der Waerden. Science Awakening II, p.149)

translated, may thus be considered a turning point in the history of Indian astrology. After that, at around the fourth century, an expansion of the work titled *Vṛddhayavanajātaka* was written (edited and published also by Pingree). This was followed by a lacuna of two centuries from which no works have survived. Despite the lack of extant texts, the astrology of Western origin seems to have attracted the attention of the Indian people. In the mid-sixth century the hiatus was put to an end by Varāhamihira.

Varāhamihira wrote an astronomical work titled *Pañcasiddhāntikā* ("[Summary of] Five Astronomical Works"). In the field of astrology, he also authored the following works:

A. Three treatises of general nature
Bṛhajjātaka—A treatise on horoscopy like the *Yavanajātaka*.
Laghujātaka—An abbreviated version of the *Bṛhajjātaka*.
Bṛhatsaṃhitā—An encyclopedic work on the traditional mantic lore.

B. Two specialized works
Bṛhadyātrā—Divination concerning royal expeditions (*yātrā*).
Vivāhapaṭala—Marriage-related divination.

The above works of Varāhamihira cover basically all the subfields within Indian astrology and remain even today the authority in their respective domains. Among these, the *Bṛhatsaṃhīta* contains materials from ancient India in addition to those of Hellenistic influences. Some of these older Indian materials may also be found in works such as the *Vedāṅga-jyotiṣa*, the *Atharvaveda-pariśiṣṭa*, the *Gargasaṃhitā*, as well as a number of older Buddhist texts.

The *Vedāṅga-jyotiṣa* is a work on calendrics (*jyotiṣa*), one of the six auxiliary disciplines (*aṅga*) associated with the Vedas. It proposes a calendar system that places two intercalary months in five years. The work contains also a detailed description of the twenty-seven *nakṣatra*-s. There are two recensions of the *Vedāṅga-jyotiṣa*, one belonging to the *Ṛgveda*, the other to the *Yajurveda*.

The Appendix (*pariśiṣṭa*) of the *Atharvaveda* begins with a section titled "Nakṣatrakalpa," which takes the twenty-eight *nakṣatra*-s as its main subject.

The *Śārdūlakarṇāvadāna* belongs to a genre of Buddhist literature known as Avadāna (didactic narratives of heroic and virtuous deeds).

This text has two early Chinese translations: i) *Modengjia jing* 摩登伽經 translated by Zhu Lüyan 竺律炎 and Zhi Qian 支謙 during the Wu Period (222–80 CE); ii) *Shetoujian taizi ershibaxiu jing* 舍頭諫太子二十八宿經 (abbr. *Shetoujian jing* 舍頭諫經) translated by Dharmarakṣa 竺法護 of Dunhuang during the Western Jin (280–316 CE). While the relation between the Sanskrit text and these two Chinese translations remains problematic, one finds in the stories of the three texts numerous descriptions related to an astrology system based on the twenty-seven or twenty-eight *nakṣatra*-s. This important work was one of the first Indian astrological texts transmitted to China through Buddhism. It was included in the Esoteric Section of the *Taishō Tripiṭaka* (Vol.21), although it was originally not an esoteric text.

The *Gargasaṃhitā* is a work ascribed to the legendary sage Garga. It is a large collection of ancient divinatory techniques. A reliable edition of the text is yet to be published. This work was frequently quoted in Utpala's commentary on the *Bṛhatsaṃhitā*.

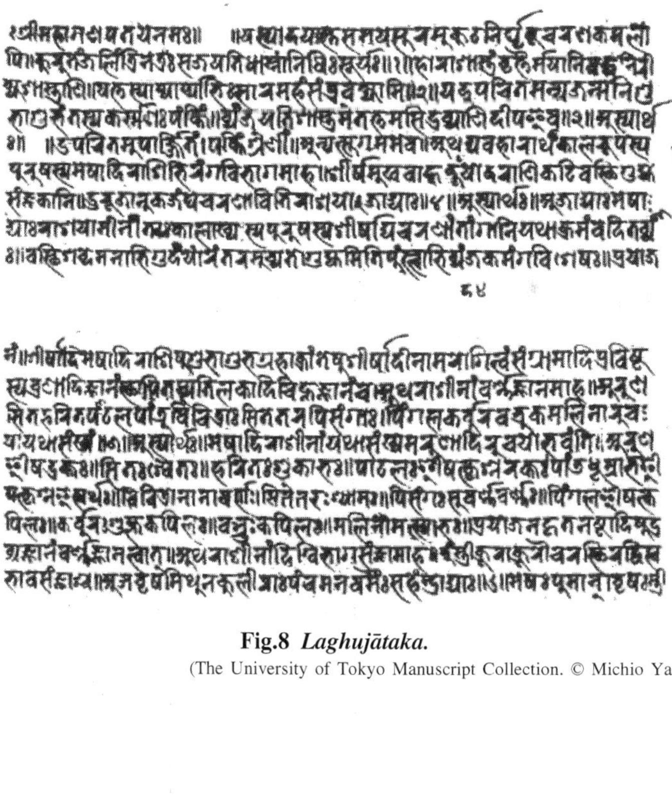

Fig.8 ***Laghujātaka.***

(The University of Tokyo Manuscript Collection. © Michio Yano)

2. Elements of New Astrology: The Relation between Planets and Days of the Week

As described earlier, the *Yavanajātaka* was among the first works to introduce new Hellenistic astrological elements to India. What is particularly noteworthy is the concept of the planetary weekdays, as well as the horoscope based on planetary positions and their interrelationship.

In Japan, the names of the days of the week are known in Japanese as *nichi* 日 (Sun), *getsu* 月 (Moon), *ka* 火 (fire), *sui* 水 (water), *moku* 木 (wood), *kin* 金 (metal), *do* 土 (earth).[10] The five planets together with the Sun and the Moon, which were considered to be planets before Copernicus, move in their own manner unlike the fixed stars. Since ancient times they were given special attention and were later deified. However, it was around the beginning of the Common Era when the planets came to represent the days of the week and were arranged in their present-day order. This order was the result of the coalescence of two concepts: i) The Greek concentric model of the universe in which spheres carrying the Sun, the Moon and the five planets move concentrically around the earth in the center; ii) the concept of the twenty-four-hour day which had originated in Egypt.

To derive the present-day order of the days of the week, one must first count the planets from the outermost planet, Saturn, as in the Greek concentric spheres model:

Saturn—Jupiter—Mars—Sun—Venus—Mercury—Moon

Each planet was thought to preside over an hour, following this order of the seven planets. It was moreover believed that for each day, the ruling planet of the first hour of a day became the ruling deity of that entire

[10] Translator's note: As in Chinese, the latter five elements correspond also to the planets Mars, Mercury, Jupiter, Venus and Saturn respectively. In English, the connection between the name of the days of the week and the planets is also somewhat evident, with Sunday, Monday, Tuesday, Wednesday, Thursday, Friday and Saturday corresponding to the Sun, the Moon, Mars, Mercury, Jupiter, Venus and Saturn respectively.

day. If one continues in this order, taking Saturn to be the ruling deity of the first day, the seventh, fourteenth and twenty-first hour of the day would belong to the Moon, and the last hour, the twenty-fourth, would go to Mars. For the following day, the ruling planet for the first hour would be the Sun (Fig.10, p.24). Thus taking the ruling deity of each day, one arrives at the following order:

Saturn—Sun—Moon—Mars—Mercury—Jupiter—Venus

Schema huius præmissæ diuisionis Sphærarum.

Fig.9 A 16th-century representation of Ptolemy's geocentric model—Universe of concentric spheres. (http://en.wikipedia.org/wiki/File:Ptolemaicsystem-small.png)

Hour/day	1	2	3	4	5	6	7
1st	Saturn	Sun	Moon	Mars	Mercury	Jupiter	Venus
2nd	Jupiter	Venus	Saturn	Sun	Moon	Mars	Mercury
3rd	Mars	Mercury	Jupiter	Venus	Saturn	Sun	Moon
4th	Sun	Moon	Mars	Mercury	Jupiter	Venus	Saturn
5th	Venus	Saturn	Sun	Moon	Mars	Mercury	Jupiter
6th	Mercury	Jupiter	Venus	Saturn	Sun	Moon	Mars
7th	Moon	Mars	Mercury	Jupiter	Venus	Saturn	Sun
...	...	...	...	...	...	...	...
21st	Moon	Mars	Mercury	Jupiter	Venus	Saturn	Sun
22nd	Saturn	Sun	Moon	Mars	Mercury	Jupiter	Venus
23rd	Jupiter	Venus	Saturn	Sun	Moon	Mars	Mercury
24th	Mars	Mercury	Jupiter	Venus	Saturn	Sun	Moon

Fig.10 The Origin of Weekday Order.

If one is to ask why our present week starts from Sunday and not Saturday, one should refer to Vettius Valens (c. mid-first century), the Roman author who was among the first to place Sunday at the start of the week. It was at around this same time when the order starting from the Sun was transmitted to India, appearing in the *Yavanajātaka* mentioned earlier. Concerning the order of weekdays, the Indian astronomer Āryabhaṭa (b.476 CE) remarked:

> saptaite horeśāḥ śanaiścarādyā yathākramaṃ śīgrāḥ |
> śīghrakramāc caturthā bhavanti sūryodayād dinapāḥ ||
> (Āryabhaṭīya 3.16)

> "These seven 'Lords of the Hour,' beginning with Saturn, are [arranged] in the order of speed [from slow to fast]. In the order of swiftness, [every] fourth becomes the 'Lord of the Day' which begins from Sunrise."

It seems that the idea of planetary gods presiding over each day was extremely novel and became popular at that time, spreading from the Mediterranean to India. It was widely adopted by the Indians, and this order of weekdays was used in all astral works after the *Yavanajātaka* when describing the planets. Even today in India, the days of the week are called by the name of the planets followed by "*-vār*" in Hindi (Skt. *-vāra*, "turn").

Thus, whenever planetary order appears in a description of the planets in any given text, one can discern how much that part of the text was influenced by the Western astrology. Dr. Makoto Zenba 善波周 of Kyoto University, who inspired my interests in the history of science in India, once examined these records in Buddhist texts and obtained the following results:[11]

Text	Edition	Planetary order (Sun as 1 etc.)
Mātaṅgasūtra 1st fasc.	*Modengjia jing* 摩登伽經卷上 (Ch. trans., mid-3rd cen. CE)	su-mo-ma-ju-sa-ve-me [1-2-3-5-7-6-4]
	Sanskrit text (Kyoto University ms.)	ve-ju-sa-me-ma-su-mo [6-5-7-4-3-1-2]
	Tibetan text (Derge)	ve-ju-sa-me-ma-su-mo [6-5-7-4-3-1-2]
Mātaṅgasūtra 2nd fasc.	*Modengjia jing* 摩登伽經卷下 (Ch. trans., mid-3rd cen. CE)	su-mo-ma-me-ju-ve-sa [1-2-3-4-5-6-7]
	Sanskrit text (Kyoto University ms.)	mo-su-ve-ju-sa-ma-me [2-1-6-5-7-3-4]
	Tibetan text (Derge)	su-mo-ju-sa-ma-me (one missing)[1-2-6-7-3-4]
Mahāsan-nipātasūtra	*Dajijing rizang fen* 大集經日藏分 (Ch. trans., late 6th cen.)	ju-ma-sa-ve-me-su-mo [5-3-7-6-4-1-2]
	Dajijing yuezang fen 大集經月藏分 (Ch. trans., late 6th cen.)	su-mo-ma-ju-sa-me-ve [1-2-3-5-7-4-6]
Mahāmāyurī-vidyārājasūtra	*Foshuo dakongque zhouwang jing* 佛說大孔雀咒王經 (Ch. trans. by Yijing 義淨, 8th cen.)	su-mo-ju-ve-sa-ma-me [1-2-5-6-7-3-4]
	Fomu dakongque mingwang jing 佛母大孔雀明王經 (Ch. trans. by Amoghavajra, 8th cen.)	su-mo-ma-me-ju-ve-sa [1-2-3-4-5-6-7] su-mo-ma-me-ju-ve-sa
	Xiuyao yigui 宿曜儀軌 (trans. by Yixing 一行, 8th cen.)	[1-2-3-4-5-6-7]
	Xiuyao jing. 2nd fasc. 宿曜經卷下 (by Amoghavajra, 8th cen.)	su-mo-ma-me-ju-ve-sa [1-2-3-4-5-6-7]
	Qiyao rangzao jue 七曜攘災决 (trans. Jinjuzha 金俱吒, 9th cen.)	su-mo-ju-ma-sa-ve-me [1-2-5-3-7-6-4]
Mañjuśrīmūla-kalpa	*Genben yigui jing* 根本儀軌經 (Ch. trans. by Tian Xizai 天息災, 10th cen.)	su-mo-ve-ju-me-ma-sa [1-2-6-5-4-3-7]
	Sanskrit text (Trivandrum)	su-mo-ma-me-ju-ve-sa [1-2-3-4-5-6-7]
	Tibetan text (Derge)	su-mo-ma-me-ju-ve-sa [1-2-3-4-5-6-7]

[11] Zenba 1956.

From the table above the following assumptions may be made. First, the order found in the two fascicles of the Chinese translations of the *Mātaṅgasūtra*, as well as that of the Sanskrit texts[12] and Tibetan recensions, are practically all different. Only that of the second fascicle of the Chinese translation of the *Mātaṅgasūtra* corresponds to the current weekday order, suggesting that it may be an interpolation. This assumption is supported by a line concerning the "intercalary months" inserted right before the description of planets in the second fascicle:

> 於十九年，凡有七閏。[13]
> "In nineteen years, there are in total seven intercalary months."

The nineteen-year cycle with seven intercalary months was known in China from around the fourth century BCE. The same was known in Mesopotamia somewhat earlier, and the famous Metonic cycle was proposed by Meton of Athens as part of the Athenian calendar in 432 BCE.[14] However, such intercalation is found in neither the Sanskrit *Śārdūlakarṇāvadāna*, nor the other Chinese translation, the *Shetoujian jing*. Therefore, one may say at least that this part of the *Mātaṅgasūtra* was interpolated into the text due to Hellenistic influence. While the relation between the Sanskrit version and these two Chinese translations is by no means clear, it is likely that somewhere in the text's process of transmission from India to China through Central Asia, this example of the latest knowledge from the West was inserted. If the order of the seven astral bodies were enumerated randomly, there would be up to 5040 possibilities—thus the pattern of the order noted above could be in no way coincidental.

While the same order of the seven luminaries is found also in the *Xiuyao jing* (not just in the second fascicle, but also the first), this is not the case in the *Qiyao rangzai jue* 七曜攘災决 ("Formulae to Prevent Disasters Caused by the Seven Luminaries"), a text of a later period. Instead, as far as the five planets are concerned, the Chinese order of Jupiter, Mars, Saturn, Venus and Mercury was adopted. Also, in the *Genben yigui jing* 根本儀軌經 (T 1191), strangely enough, part of the standard planetary order which was found in the Sanskrit recension, namely, "Mars-Mercury-Jupiter-Venus" was reversed.

---

[12] Translator's note: Zenba consulted only the Kyoto University manuscript, before the Mukhopadhyaya edition was published.

[13] Taishō(1300)21.410a.

[14] See p.99.

In China, apart from the Sun and the Moon, it is customary for the five planets to be called *Yinghuo* 熒惑, *Chenxing* 辰星, *Suixing* 歲星, *Taibai* 太白 and *Zhuensing* 鎮星, with which the five elements were associated, namely Fire, Water, Wood, Metal and Earth respectively. In the minds of the Chinese, these names, however, have no connection with the days of the week, as they do for the Japanese. The concept of planetary weekdays came to China from the West shortly before the advent of the *Xiuyao jing* and was popular only during a relatively short period of time.

As it will be shown later, the use of the character "*mi*" (蜜 or 密) was transmitted to Japan through the *Xiuyao jing*. The radical 𠮷, as well as "mitsu" みつ and "michi" みち in hiragana are found also in old Japanese almanacs known as *Guchūreki* 具注暦. This character originates from *mīr/myr* in Sogdian, a middle Iranian language, whose cognate *mihir* in Pahlavī, a middle Persian language, is in fact *mithra* in the older language. *Mithra* is the name of the solar deity.

It was the Manichaeans who brought this Sogdian word *mīr* to China. For the Manichaeans, Sunday was considered a special day. Manichaeism was a religion founded in third-century Iran, as a mélange of doctrines from Zoroastrianism, Christianity, Buddhism and Gnosticism. Due to persecution by the Zoroastrians, the Manicheans fled to the East and their religion spread in particular to the Uighur people in Central Asia. The Uighur were the ones who brought Manichaeism to China.

It is interesting that the Japanese continued to use the loanword "*mitsu*" or "*michi*," just as the Uighurs borrowed the names of weekdays from the Sogdians.

Currently, we have all taken for granted that Sunday is the rest day. In our modern calendar, it is customary to show Sunday in red. Such custom was in fact practiced by some Japanese as early as the Heian Period (794–1185 CE).

3. Advent of Horoscope and Genethliacal Astrology

Let us now briefly examine another new element that was transmitted to India from the West, namely, genethliacal astrology based on the casting of horoscopes. The positions of the Sun, the Moon and the five planets, as well as their interrelationships, are vital to the casting of horoscopes. However, to indicate the positions of the planets, whose movements are irregular, it is necessary to establish some kind of coordinate system. It is in Mesopotamia that we find the first instance of the twelve zodiacal signs used as coordinates. The horoscope of 410 BCE, which we mentioned earlier shows the close relationship between astrology and mathematical astronomy from the very beginning. The twelve zodiacal signs are defined as the ecliptic (the Sun's course) divided into twelve equal parts, each consisting of thirty degrees. Since their names are mostly identical to the names of the Mesopotamian constellations, their Mesopotamian origin may be assumed. However, since Hipparchus of Rhodes discovered the precession of equinoxes, the ecliptic coordinates that commence at the spring equinox are known to be moving westward against the fixed stars. As a result, as a set of ecliptic coordinates the twelve zodiacal signs become slightly displaced from the actual constellations each year which we shall discuss further in the following section. For now, let us compare their names in English (as derived from Latin), Japanese, Sanskrit (or as translated in the *Xiuyao jing*), and modern Chinese (Fig.12).

Fig.11 Babylonian (Seleucid period) planetary ephemeris (Jupiter).

Sign	English	Japanese	Sanskrit	*Xiuyao jing*	Modern Chinese
♈	Aries	ohitsuji	meṣa	羊宮	白羊宮
♉	Taurus	oushi	vṛṣa	牛宮	金牛宮
♊	Gemini	futago	mithuna	夫妻宮 (男女宮)	雙子宮
♋	Cancer	kani	karkaṭa	蟹宮	巨蟹宮
♌	Leo	shishi	siṃha	獅子宮	獅子宮
♍	Virgo	otome	kanyā	女宮	處女宮
♎	Libra	tenbin	tulā	秤宮	天秤宮
♏	Scorpio	sasori	vṛścika	蝎宮	天蝎宮
♐	Sagittarius	ite	dhanus (dhanvin)	弓宮	人馬宮
♑	Capricorn	yagi	makara (mṛga)	摩竭宮	摩羯宮
♒	Aquarius	mizugame	kumbha	瓶宮	寶瓶宮
♓	Pisces	uo	mīna	魚宮	雙魚宮

Fig.12 Names of Twelve Zodiacal signs.

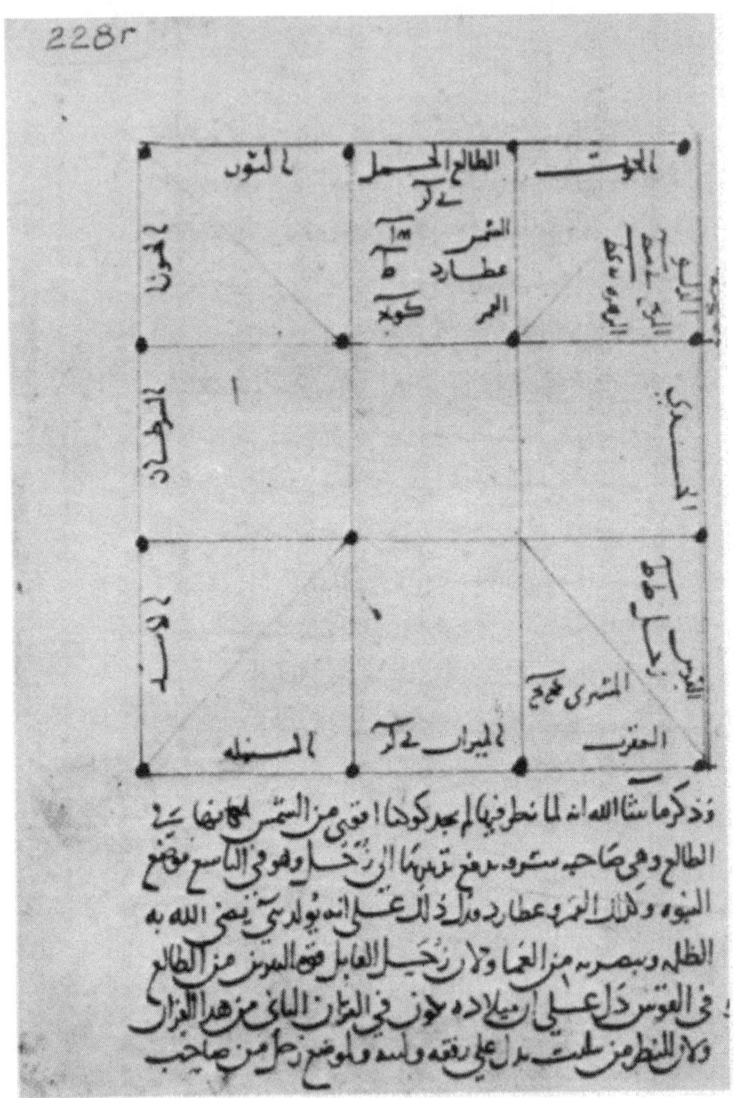

Fig.13 A Horoscope (Islamic Period).

Fig.14 Sagittarius (from Hevelius' Star Atlas *Firmamentum Sobiescianum*).

(http://nrm.wikipedia.org/wiki/File:Sagittarius_Hevelius.jpg)

Fig.15 Gemini (from Islamic source).

(http://www.grouporigin.com/clients/qatarfoundation/photos/chapter2/photo_11_big.jpg)

Fig.16 Sinicized Gemini—"Zodiacal sign of Man and Woman" 男女宮
(*Butsuzōzui* 仏像図彙).

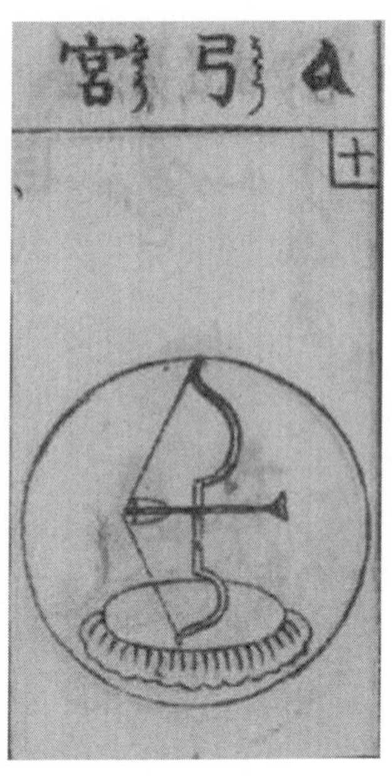

Fig.17 Sinicized Sagittarius—"Zodiacal sign of Bow" 弓宮
(*Butsuzōzui* 仏像図彙).

Fig.18 Sinicized Capricorn—"Zodiacal sign of Makara" 摩羯宮
(*Butsuzōzui* 仏像図彙).

Iconographically speaking, the representations of the zodiacal signs correspond largely to each other across different traditions. However, some variations may be observed. First, while Gemini refers to the male twins in the West, it was transformed into a couple (man and woman) in Sanskrit, a form adopted in the *Xiuyao jing* (man and woman, or husband and wife) as well. As for Sagittarius, while both forms in Sanskrit, *dhanvin* (bow-bearer) and *dhanus* (bow) are found, the *Xiuyao jing* adopts only the latter. In a Dunhuang mural, Sagittarius was represented as a man standing next to a horse, reflecting a misinterpretation of the Chinese translation of centaur, *renma* 人馬 (literally "man-horse"). Capricorn was depicted as having the head of a goat and the body of a fish-monster (sinicized as in Fig.18). In Sanskrit, this zodiacal sign is called *mṛga* (deer) or *makara* (crocodile). *Mojie* 摩竭 (Jp.*makatsu*) in the *Xiuyao jing* is a transliteration of the latter in Sanskrit.

Indian Zodiac and Western Zodiac

The Western and the Indian zodiacal signs do not correspond exactly to each other astronomically. As we have seen earlier, the spring equinox shifts from east to west on the ecliptic about 50" every year due to precession. Or as Hipparchus posited, taking the spring equinox as a fixed point, the sidereal sphere rotates from west to east. Since the Western ecliptic coordinates have adopted this shifting spring equinox as its starting point, the position of the tropical zodiacal signs continues to drift apart against the actual stars. At around 300 CE when Hellenistic astronomy was introduced to India, Indian astronomers fixed the starting point of the ecliptic coordinates at the spring equinox at that time, that is, *meṣādi* (0° of Aries). After that, the backward motion of the spring equinox caused by precession was not taken into consideration. As a result, presently the Indian ecliptic coordinates diverge by approximately 24° from those of the Western system. As shown in Fig.19, since the starting point of the Indian coordinates, Aries (*meṣādi*), is about 24° away from the actual spring equinox, the Sun arrives at that point only at around April 14 in the current Western calendar. In India, the entry of the Sun into a new zodiacal sign is called *saṃkrānti*. Important festivals take place on the four *saṃkrānti*-s, that is, the equinoxes and solstices. The *makara-saṃkrānti*, that is, when the Sun enters Capricorn, was originally winter solstice festival. For the reason mentioned above, it is now celebrated at around January 15 in the Western calendar.

Due to the difference between the Western (tropical) and the Indian (sidereal) zodiac, a person born on April 6 would belong to Aries, or the sign of the Goat in the Western system, but to the sign of the Fish (*Pisces*) in the Indian one. In five hundred years' time, the difference will grow one zodiacal sign further. This discrepancy between the spring equinox and the starting point of the Indian zodiac is known as *ayana* (precession) in Sanskrit. Divination that makes use of pure Indian zodiacal signs without precession is known as *nirayana*, while that which makes use of the coordinates of the Western zodiac is known as *sāyana*. In Indian astrology, whether one adopts the *nirayana* or the *sāyana* method would naturally make a substantial difference. As far as the current Indian almanacs I have consulted, almost all belong to the *nirayana* system.[15]

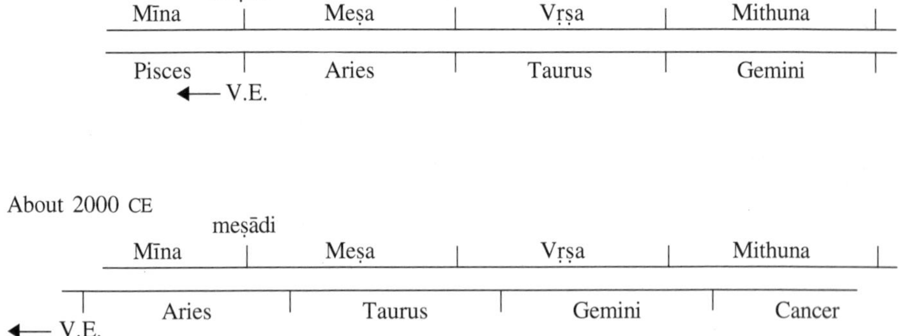

Fig.19 Difference between Indian Zodiac and Western Zodiac.

In the first figure above the initial points of ecliptic coordinates are the same, while in about 2000 CE, as shown in the second figure below, the western Vernal Equinox shifted to the left by about 24 degrees.

---

[15] In Western horoscopy, the sidereal system was also proposed along with the more popular tropic system.

Origin of the "Twelve Places"

Among the fundamental elements in horoscopy is the concept of "place."[16] It is defined by the relationship between the celestial sphere, which makes one rotation daily, and the horizon. Starting from the point where the ecliptic intersects with the eastern horizon when the horoscope is cast, the celestial sphere is then divided into twelve equal parts of 30° each along the equator in the direction of increasing ecliptic longitude—or in other words, in the opposite direction against the daily rotation of the celestial sphere.

Fig.20 shows how the Twelve Places are projected onto the equator.[17] The plane occupied by the Twelve Places is 24° inclined against the ecliptic plane.

The origin of the Twelve Places in fact is dated relatively late. The places corresponding to positions I, IV, VII and X appear to have been given special attention in around the second century BCE, and were gradually developed into the Twelve Places. Sextos Empeirikos of the latter half of the second century CE described the problem quite extensively in his "Against the Astrologers," the fifth chapter of *Against the Professors*. While this may give the impression that the Twelve Places described in the text enjoyed some popularity at that time, no detailed description on the subject was given in Ptolemy's *Tetrabiblos* which immediately predated it.

In India some of the basic concepts of the Twelve Places are described in the *Yavanajātaka*. It is interesting to note that many of the Sanskrit technical terms in the work are in fact transliterations from Greek. In Varāhamihira's *Bṛhajjātaka*, the Twelve Places are translated by their semantic value for the first time. In Greek, the word for "place" is *tópos*, which means "location," and in Latin, it is *domus*, which means "home." In Sanskrit, the word for zodiacal sign, *rāśi*, is distinct from other words such as *gṛha* ("house"), *bhāva* ("state") and *sthāna* ("place"). Among the Buddhist astrological works translated into Chinese, the *Quiyao rangzai jue*, dated slightly after the *Xiuyao jing*, is the first text to mention the Twelve Places, which are called *gong* 宫 (Jp., *kyū* "mansion"), the same term for the zodiacal signs. In Japan, the

[16] Translator's note: I have avoided the term "house" here because it is also used sometimes to refer to the signs.

[17] In fact, the two planes are inclined against each other.

zodiacal sign (*kyū* 宮) is clearly distinguished from the "place" (*i* 位) only after around the mid-Heian Period.

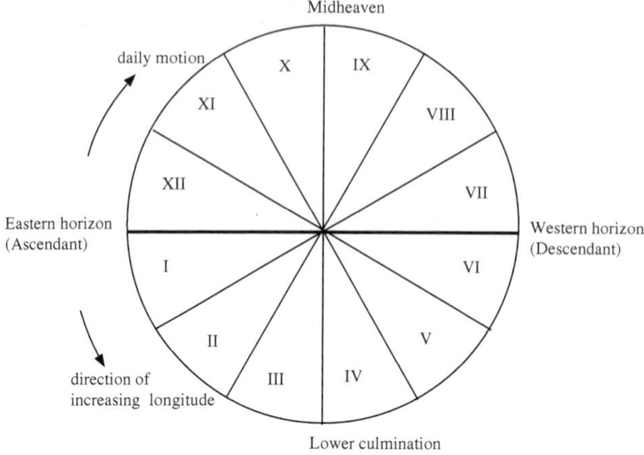

Fig.20 Twelve Places.

Place	West	India	Iran	*Qiyao rangzai jue*
I	life, body	*tanu* (body)	*gyānān* (life)	命宮 (place/house of life)
II	wealth	*dhana* (wealth)	*kīsagān* (wealth)	財宮 (place/house of wealth)
III	siblings	*sahaja* (sibiling)	*brādarān* (brother)	兄弟 (brothers)
IV	parents	*suhṛt/bandhava* (friend/relative)	*pedištān* (dwelling)	田宅 (land property)
V	offspring	*suta* (offspring)	*frazandān* (offspring)	男女 (offspring)
VI	servants, sickness, foes	*ripu* (foe)	*waštagān* (patient)	僮僕 (servants)
VII	marriage	*jāyā* (wife)	*wayodagān* (marriage couple)	妻妾/夫妻 (wives/spouse)
VIII	death	*mṛtyu* (death)	*margān* (death/dead person)	疾病/病厄 (sickness)
IX	friendship, travel	dharma	*kārdāgān* (travel/traveler)	遷移 (movement/relocation)
X	fame, position	*karma/āspada* (action/power)	*mayān ī asmān* (middle of sky)	官位 (career)
XI	friends, welfare	*āya* (gain)	*farroxān* (fortune)	福相 (fortune)
XII	foes, misfortune	*vyaya* (loss)	*dušfarragān* (misfortune)	困窮/禍害 (poverty/misfortune)

Fig.21 Comparison of the Twelve Places in the *Qiyao rangzai jue* and other sources.

In the table (Fig.21), the corresponding meanings for the Twelve Places in the *Qiyao rangzai jue* as from the West, India and Iran, respectively, are given. They correspond largely to one another with the exception of IV. Itō Gikyō 伊藤義教 points out that the names of the Twelve Places used in the Japanese horoscopes are particularly close to those in Pahlavī.[18] The Japanese names for the Twelve Places came from the *Qiyao rangzai jue*, which is closely related to the *Futian li* 符天曆.[19]

In Greek, *hōroskopos*, meaning the observation of the "first place" on the eastern horizon, is the origin of the English word "horoscope." The first part of the Greek word ὥρα, which corresponds to the modern English word "hour," is the division of a day into twenty-four parts. The word ὥρα was transmitted to India early (to become *horā* in Sanskrit) and had come to mean the degrees of sidereal rotation in one hour, or in other words, 15°, or half a zodiacal sign. In the Chinese Tripiṭaka, there is a text titled the *Fantian huoluo jiuyao* 梵天火羅九曜 (T.1311) in which *huoluo* is none other the Chinese transliteration for *horā*.

What Is a Horoscope?

Let us define what a horoscope is. A horoscope is not necessarily always in the form of a diagram we now commonly expect. On the clay tablets found in Babylonia, the horoscopes are often expressed in cuneiform as simply text records of planetary positions. The earliest extant horoscope in a diagram format is dated to the first century CE, and is written in Greek. The planetary positions of this horoscope are not clear enough to suggest the exact date. It has, however, been roughly dated to around the time of the Roman Emperor Tiberius (reign 14–37 CE).[20] The planetary positions are first described in the text, followed by the diagram. A hand-copied version of the chart in Neugebauer and Van Hoesen [1959] and an English translation are given as follows (Figs.22–1, 22–2).

In Fig.22–1, although all the twelve zodiacal signs are noted, the names of the Twelve Places are not found. Instead, out of the four cardinals, only three points, namely, the ascendant, the zenith and the nadir, are indicated. It is customary for the ascendant—in other words, the ecliptic point on the eastern horizon—to face left. While the Greek

[18] Itō 1980.

[19] See § 5.5, pp.143–44.

[20] Neugebauer and Van Hoesen 1959.

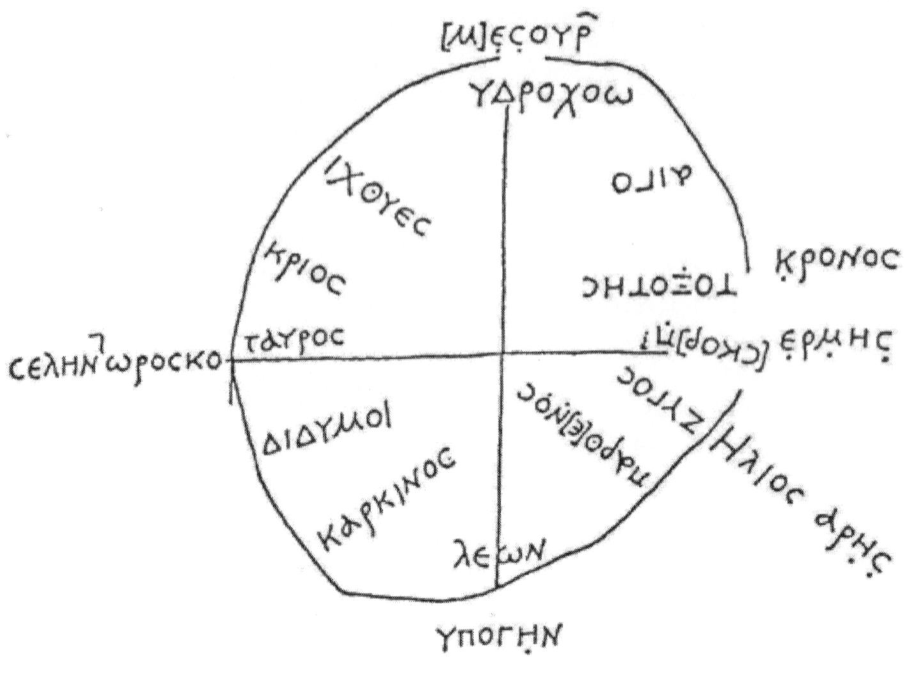
[Μ]ΕϹΟΥΡ
ΥΔΡΟΧΟΩ
ΙΧΘΥΕϹ
ΚΡΙΟϹ
ΤΑΥΡΟϹ
ϹΕΛΗΝΗ ΩΡΟϹΚΟ
ΔΙΔΥΜΟΙ
ΚΑΡΚΙΝΟϹ
ΛΕΩΝ
ΥΠΟΓΗΝ
ΚΡΟΝΟϹ
ΕΡΜΗϹ
ΖΥΓΟϹ
ΗΛΙΟϹ ΑΡΗϹ

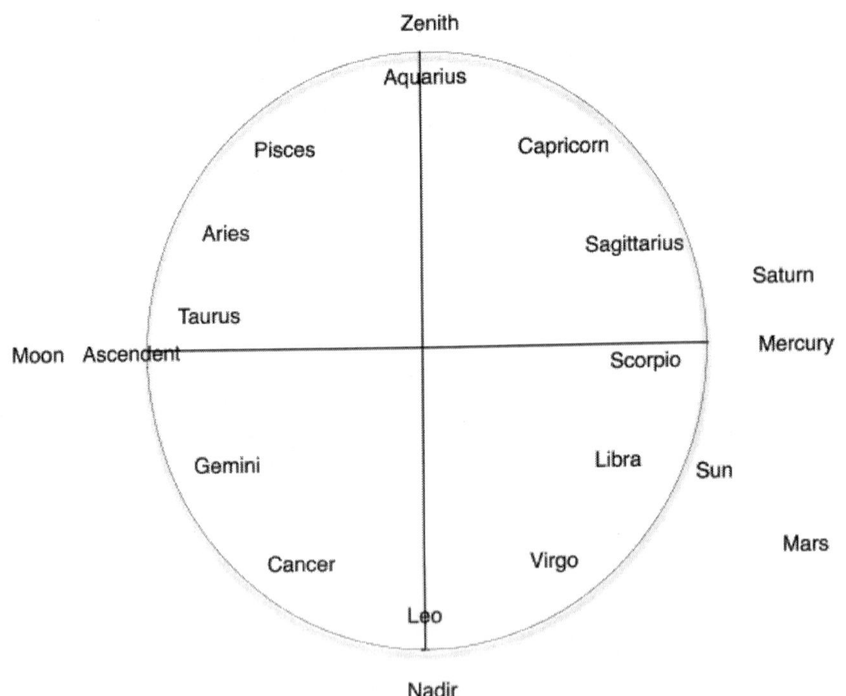
Zenith
Aquarius
Pisces
Capricorn
Aries
Sagittarius
Saturn
Taurus
Moon
Ascendent
Mercury
Scorpio
Gemini
Libra
Sun
Mars
Cancer
Virgo
Leo
Nadir

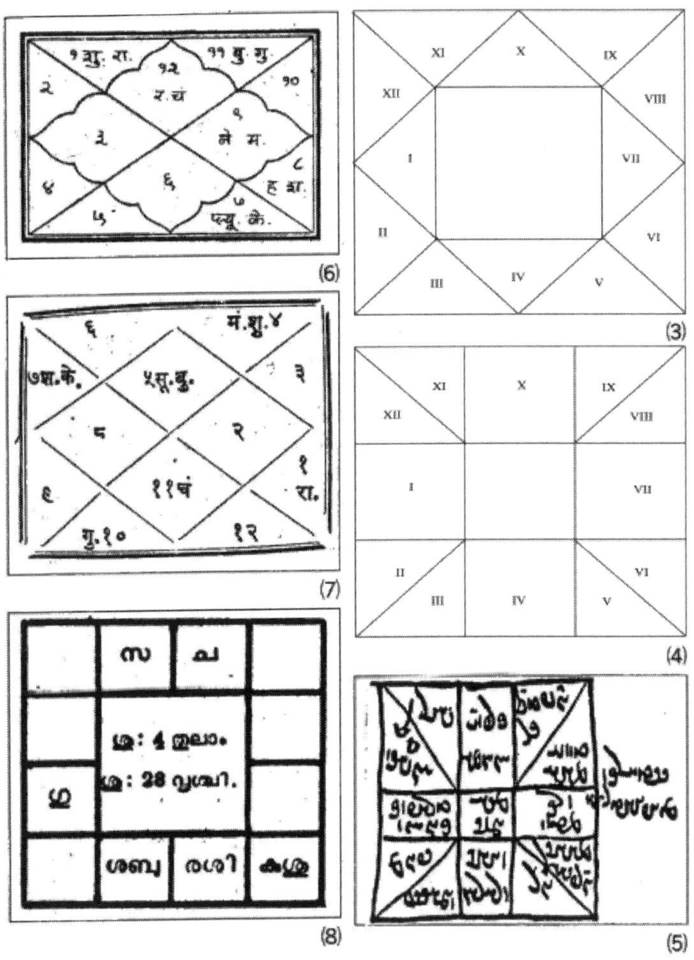

Fig.22 Horoscopes from (1) the Early Hellenistic World with translation (2), (3)/(4) Medieval Europe, (5) Medieval Persia, (6)–(8) Modern India.

horoscope diagrams are circular in shape, horoscopes in medieval Europe are square. In Figs.22–3 and 22–4, the square is divided from the first (I) to the twelfth places (XII), and the positions of the planets at the time of birth are written inside the small squares.

Many of the Iranian horoscopes resemble that of Fig.22–4. If we turn the chart 90 degrees clockwise, the first place (ascendant) would be at the top. An example is found in a Zoroastrian text called *Bundahišn*, written in Pahlavi (Fig.22–5). This chart is not a horoscope cast for an individual's birth, rather it was described as a "world horoscope" (*thema mundi*), or a horoscope of the world when it came into existence. In this chart, instead of the Twelve Places, the names of the twelve signs are written, together with the planetary positions. In the text, the "Place of Life," or the "ascendant" is Cancer, where Jupiter is positioned. Cancer (Persian: *Karzang*) may be seen at the top center of the diagram.

What, then, do the Indian horoscopes look like? Unfortunately, I am not aware of the existence of any old horoscopes in India. In some local almanacs, charts such as those in Figs.22–6, 22–7 and 22–8 may be found, and they are all square in shape. A chart drawn by the lecturer at an astrology seminar held in Trivandrum, Kerala, is given here (Fig.22–8).[21] This seems to be a typical horoscope from southern India. The direction of the "signs" is presented clockwise, in contrast to the more common anticlockwise horoscopes.

One of the examples of horoscopes transmitted to China is the *Zhengshi xing'an* 鄭氏星案. According to Prof. Yabuuti Kiyosi, it dates to the Tang Period. As shown in Fig.25, the diagram is dodecagonal. If converted to a round shape, it would look just like the horoscope used by Japanese astrologers (Figs.49, 51). The Japanese horoscopes are radial in shape, divided into twelve parts of thirty degrees each. The eastern horizon is oriented to the nine o'clock position and the part immediately below the horizon thus becomes the ascendant, which is called the "Place of Life" 壽命位. From here, the names of the Twelve Places are written counterclockwise. In the inner circle are the names of the twenty-eight *xiu-s* 宿, referring to either the Indian *nakṣatra*-s or the Chinese lodges. The gridded space in between is used to indicate the planetary positions. In the innermost circle, the twelve branches 十二支 of indigenous Chinese origin are written clockwise.

Astrology and Astronomy

Among the various forms of astrology, genethliacal astrology came about the latest due to the late development of the mathematical astronomy which is its foundation. At localities of the same latitude, the celestial equator always crosses the horizon at the same angle; to calculate at what angle the ecliptic crosses the horizon and the

[21] Translator's note: Yano's visit to Kerala is described in Chapter six of the Japanese edition, which is translated only partially in this book.

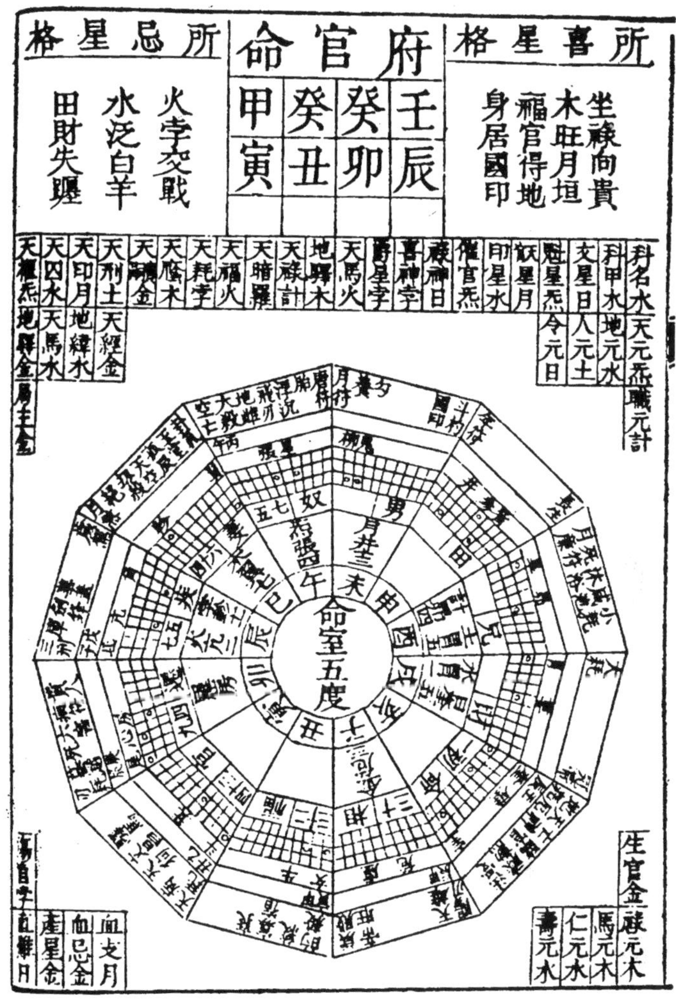

Fig.22(9) ***Zhengshi xing'an*** **鄭氏星案 (Chinese Horoscope).**

meridian, knowledge of spherical geometry is necessary. Thus, mathematical astronomy and astrology developed hand-in-hand. In Greece, Hipparchus was the one who first solved this problem by projecting the spherical surface onto a plane; in the first century CE, Menelaos discovered spherical trigonometry. However, Menelaos's method did not reach India, and instead Hipparchus's method of stereographic projection became the basis for subsequent development in Indian astronomy.

The calculation of planetary longitudes is more complicated. One may say that Greek astronomy up to Ptolemy was primarily concerned with this problem; however, the planetary theory transmitted to India belongs to the period before Ptolemy. Subsequently, the Indian theory and computational technique developed in its own way.

With respect to Esoteric Buddhist astrological texts, unfortunately, almost none of the mathematical aspects of Indian astrology and astronomy are included, with the single exception of the *Qiyao rangzai jue*. This work is mostly made up of tables showing planetary positions. While it is not clear by which method these tables were computed, it is nonetheless apparent that they were used for the computation of planetary positions, which were essential for horoscope-making.[22]

Chapter Two—Additional Notes

(1) On the date of the *Yāvanajātaka*

As the first work of Greek astrology transmitted to India, the *Yāvanajātaka* edited and published by Pingree was undoubtedly a work of great importance. However, recently new findings concerning the date of this work have come to light. In 2011, together with my postgraduate student Sho Hirose, I discovered by sheer chance a new manuscript of the *Yavanajātaka* in the catalogue of the National Archives in Kathmandu. Written on paper instead of palm leaves, the manuscript is relatively recent, though it belongs to a tradition different from that of the manuscript Pingree used. It was probably unknown to Pingree when he conducted his research. On the last page of this manuscript, a portion corresponding to the colophon of the work was found. Upon examination, Bill Mak discovered that the dates appearing in Pingree's edition were in fact not written as such in the manuscript. A closer examination of the manuscript used by Pingree revealed that Pingree's reading was erroneous. Details on the matter are discussed in Mak's 2013 papers.[23] For now, suffice it to say that there is no evidence to suggest that the versification of the *Yavanajātaka* took place in 269 CE. Moreover, the claim that the "original prose version" was composed in 150 CE is mere conjecture. These dates for the

[22] Yano 1995:73. See §5.2. P.122.

[23] Mak 2013a, 2013b.

Yavanajātaka were reproduced by Pingree in all his works and monographs. I, myself, for many years had followed suit. From now on these dates should be revised, although I would refrain from giving a precise date. What can be said with confidence, is that the first prose version of the work was composed by Yavaneśvara, a king of Greek lineage in a West Indian colony, some time around the third or fourth century. The work that we have now was probably versified by another person who was known as Sphujidhvaja. The relationship between these two individuals is unclear.

(2) On Varāhamihira's *Bṛhatsaṃhitā*

Since I was young I have been deeply interested in this work. When I had the opportunity to give a seminar at the Faculty of Letters, Kyoto University, I chose this text for the lecture. Mizue Sugita, then a graduate student, participated in my class with great enthusiasm and offered to translate the text into Japanese with me. As a result, a Japanese translation was published.[24] This work is extremely interesting, as it contains two kinds of astrology, one which I call "lunar astrology"; the other is generally known as the new astrology of Western origin. This text provides us many hints for understanding the astrology of Esoteric Buddhism.

(3) About the *Śārdūlakarṇāvadāna*

With regard to this work and its two Chinese translations, recently I had an opportunity to study them with Zhou Liqun 周利群 from Peking University. Zhou participated in the research seminar of the International Research Institute for Advanced Buddhology of Soka University and is currently comparing Sanskrit fragments excavated in Central Asia with the two Chinese translations. As it turns out, the Central Asian manuscript has a very important role in the study of sinicized Buddhist astrology. For example, the *nakṣatra* Kṛttikā was translated as *mingcheng* 名稱 (lit., "name" or "fame") in the *Shetoujian jing*. In my previous work, I had pointed out that this was due to a misunderstanding of the etymology of Kṛttikā as if it was derived from *kīrti*;[25] however, it turned out that the word *kīrti* was in fact found in the Central Asian

[24] Yano and Sugita 1995.

[25] Yano 2004:118.

manuscript. In the case of the lunar lodge *Wei* 危, it was translated as *baidu xiu* 百毒宿 ("lodge of hundred poisons"). The manuscript in fact gives the reading *Śataviṣa* ("hundred poisons") instead of *Śatabhiṣaj* ("hundred physicians"). Such examples have made me realize the important role Central Asia played in the historical transmission of astral science from India to China. Materials related to the Sanskrit manuscripts from Central Asia were published by the aforementioned research institute.[26]

(4) On the Chinese Translation of the Twelve Zodiacal Signs

The first Chinese translation of the twelve Western zodiacal signs is found in the Buddhist text *Dajijing* 大集經. Within this voluminous work, detailed astrological materials are found in two chapters, namely, the *Sūryagarbha-parivarta* and the *Candragarbha-parivarta* translated by Narendrayaśas of the Sui Dynasty.[27] The names of the zodiacal signs found in the *Sūryagarbha-parivarta* were translated instead of transliterated: Aries > *chiyang zhi shen* 持羊之神 ("goat-holding deity"), Taurus > *chiniu zhi shen* 持牛之神 ("cow-holding deity"), Gemini > *shuangniao zhi shen* 雙鳥之神 ("double birds deity"), Cancer > *xie shen* 蟹神 ("crab deity), Leo > *shizi zhi shen* 師子之神 ("lion deity"), Virgo > *tiannü zhi shen*) 天女之神 ("heavenly maiden deity"), Libra > *pingliang zhi shen* 秤量之神 ("balance deity"), Scorpio > *xie shen* 蝎神 ("scorpion deity"), Sagittarius > *she shen* 射神 ("shooting deity"), Capricorn > *mojie zhi shen* 磨竭之神 ("*makara* deity"), Aquarius > *shuiqi zhi shen* 水器之神 ("deity of water vessel"), Pisces > *tianyu zhi shen* 天魚之神 ("heavenly fish deity"). It seems to me strange that Gemini was made into "a pair of birds" instead of either two twin males (as in the West) or the male-female couple (as in India).

(5) On the *Fantian huoluo jiuyao* 梵天火羅九曜

This Buddhist work was ascribed to the Chan Master Yixing 一行. Yixing (683–727 CE) excelled in mathematical astronomy and is well known as the author of the calendar *Dayan li* 大衍曆. Yixing is also one of the eight patriarchs of the Mantra (Shingon) School. The *huoluo* from the title is in

[26] Miyazaki, Nagashima, Tami and Zhou (2015).

[27] The Chinese translations of the two chapters were known also independently as the "Rizang pin" 日藏品 (**Sūryagarbha-sūtra*) and "Yuezang pin" 月藏品 (**Candragarbha-sūtra*) respectively. I have included the Chinese phonetic transliteration of the twelve zodiacal signs found in the **Candragarbha-parivarta* as a list in Yano 2004:123.

fact a phonetic transliteration of the Sanskrit word *horā*, which was in turn derived from Greek. In India, horoscopic astrology was called *horā-śāstra*, or in other words, the science of *horā*. The text *Fantian huoluo jiuyao* describes which age was governed by which of the nine luminaries, that is, the seven luminaries together with Rāhu and Ketu. It includes also the mantras, offerings and iconography to be used in the ritual offerings to the deities of the nine luminaries. Some of the wordings and the iconography are reflected in the scroll painting *Karazu* 火羅図 kept in the Tōji Temple in Kyoto. This noteworthy scroll painting is basically Esoteric Buddhist Astrology in a nutshell, mixed with some Chinese elements. A color copy of the work is reproduced as the frontispiece of Yano 2004.

(6) On Horoscope Diagrams

For the "World Horoscope" found in the *Bundahišn*, a Zoroastrian text from medieval Persia, see Chapter Five of Yano 2004. On pp.78–80, I described the similarity between this horoscope and the one for Rāma's birth found at the beginning of the *Rāmāyana*, the Indian epic. In this work, one can see the influence from the Indian sense of direction, which regards the East as the "front" and west as the "back." In the horoscope of the *Bundahišn*, the positions of the head and the tail of the Gōzihr ("dragon") are given. On the other hand, in Rāma's horoscope the corresponding Rāhu and Ketu are not found. Rāhu and Ketu in Esoteric Buddhist astrology are discussed in greater detail in Section 5.3.

The Japanese horoscope mentioned in Chapter Five places the ascendent at the nine o'clock position, as in Western examples. The reason for this should be examined. Furthermore, while the Twelve Places are positioned counter-clockwise in most horoscopes, they are positioned clockwise in South Indian horoscopes. An example of the latter may be found in Fig.22(8).

III. CONTENTS OF *XIUYAO JING*

In this chapter, the contents of the *Xiuyao jing* will be discussed in detail. As already mentioned, the order of the two fascicles of the work was inverted in the Continental edition. There is moreover an additional section in the Japanese manuscripts. I shall examine the text in the order of the six chapters, plus the additional section. Correspondences and differences with the second fascicle will be noted accordingly. The Kakushō edition is used here as our source text.

1. Relationship between Twenty-seven *Nakṣatra*-s and Twelve Zodiacal Signs

The topic of the first chapter of the *Xiuyao jing* is a description of the relationship between the twenty-seven *nakṣatra*-s and the twelve zodiacal signs (*gong* 宫 or *rāśi*-s).

The term *xiu* 宿, "lunar lodge" in Chinese, corresponds to the Indian concept of *nakṣatra*, or "lunar mansion." The Moon goes once around the celestial sphere from west to east in about 27.3 days. The group of bright stars through which the Moon passes each day is called a *xiu*. Similar concepts are also found in Indian and Arabic texts and their origin has long been a subject of debate. Irrespective of their origin, the stars that constitute the asterisms of these three civilizations are not necessarily identical. For example, in contrast to the twenty-eight "lodges" of China, both twenty-seven and twenty-eight *nakṣatra*-s are found in India. In the case of the twenty-seven *nakṣatra* system, it can either refer to the twenty-seven stars or groups of stars, or more broadly, a division of the ecliptic into twenty-seven equal parts, or 13°20'. This is essential to our understanding of the twenty-seven *nakṣatra*-s described in the first chapter of the *Xiuyao jing*. The twenty-seven Indian *nakṣatra*-s are replaced by the corresponding twenty-seven Chinese lodges for convenience, excluding the Chinese lodge *Niu* 牛. The relationship between the twenty-seven Indian *nakṣatra*-s and their Chinese translations is shown below in Fig.23.

In this system, the twenty-seven *nakṣatra*-s are divided into two groups: firstly, thirteen and a half *nakṣatra*-s from *Maghā* (10. *Xing* 星) to the first half of *Dhaniṣṭhā* (23. *Xu* 虚) are assigned to the Sun; then,

Division		Indian Name	Chinese Equivalents	
lunar	1	Aśvinī	婁	lóu
	2	Bharaṇī	胃	wèi
	3	Kṛttikā	昴	mǎo
	4	Rohiṇī	畢	bì
	5	Mṛgaśīrṣa	觜	zī
	6	Ārdrā	參	shēn
	7	Punarvasū	井	jǐng
	8	Puṣya	鬼	guǐ
	9	Āśleṣā	柳	liǔ
solar	10	Maghā	星	xīng
	11	Pūrvaphalgunī	張	zhāng
	12	Uttaraphalgunī	翼	yì
	13	Hasta	軫	zhên
	14	Citrā	角	jiǎo
	15	Svāti	亢	kàng
	16	Viśākhā	氐	dī
	17	Anurādhā	房	fáng
	18	Jyeṣṭhā	心	xīn
	19	Mūla	尾	wěi
	20	Pūrvāṣāḍhā	箕	jī
	21	Uttarāṣāḍhā	斗	dǒu
	22	Śravaṇa	女	nü
	23	Dhaniṣṭhā	虛	xū
lunar	24	Śatabhiṣaj	危	wēi
	25	Pūvabhādrapadā	室	shì
	26	Uttarabhādrapadā	壁	bì
	27	Revatī	奎	kuí

Fig.23 Twenty-seven Indian *nakṣatra*-s and their Chinese equivalents.

the remaining thirteen and a half *nakṣatra*-s from *Āśleṣa* (9. *Liu* 柳) going opposite to the second half of *Dhaniṣṭhā* are assigned to the Moon. Incidentally, in the Continental edition, the description of the thirteen and a half *nakṣatra*-s belonging to the Moon is missing by haplology. This is what prompted me to look for other better manuscripts of the text.

In the same way, the twelve signs are separated into solar and lunar divisions with six zodiacal signs each. Leo, which starts the solar division, becomes the sign of the Sun, while the remaining five signs are assigned to the five planets accordingly. Cancer, which starts the lunar division, becomes the sign of the Moon and the rest of the five signs are similarly assigned to the five planets, but in reverse order. One should note that the order of these planets is based on that of the Greek concentric model described earlier (pp.22–23).

As for the relationship between the twelve zodiacal signs and the twenty-seven *nakṣatra*-s, each zodiacal sign occupies two and a quarter *nakṣatra*-s (27÷12 = 2¼). In the *Xiuyao jing*, the quarter unit is called a foot, *zu* 足 (Skt. *pāda*), and thus one sign consists of nine *zu*-s (*pāda*-s). The text describes the relationship between the *nakṣatra*-s and their corresponding zodiacal signs, summarized here as Fig.24.

Solar Division 太陽分	Sun	Leo	星 4/4	張 4/4	翼 1/4
	Mercury	Virgo	翼 3/4	軫 4/4	角 2/4
	Venus	Libra	角 2/4	亢 4/4	氐 3/4
	Mars	Scorpio	氐 1/4	房 4/4	心 4/4
	Jupiter	Sagittarius	尾 4/4	箕 4/4	箕 1/4
	Saturn	Capricorn	斗 3/4	女 4/4	虛 2/4
Lunar Division 太陰分	Saturn	Aquarius	虛 2/4	危 4/4	室 3/4
	Jupiter	Pisces	室 1/4	壁 4/4	奎 4/4
	Mars	Aries	婁 4/4	胃 4/4	昴 1/4
	Venus	Taurus	昴 3/4	畢 4/4	觜 2/4
	Mercury	Gemini	觜 2/4	參 4/4	井 3/4
	Moon	Cancer	井 1/4	鬼 4/4	柳 4/4

Fig.24 Twelve Zodiacal signs and Twenty-seven *nakṣatra*-s.

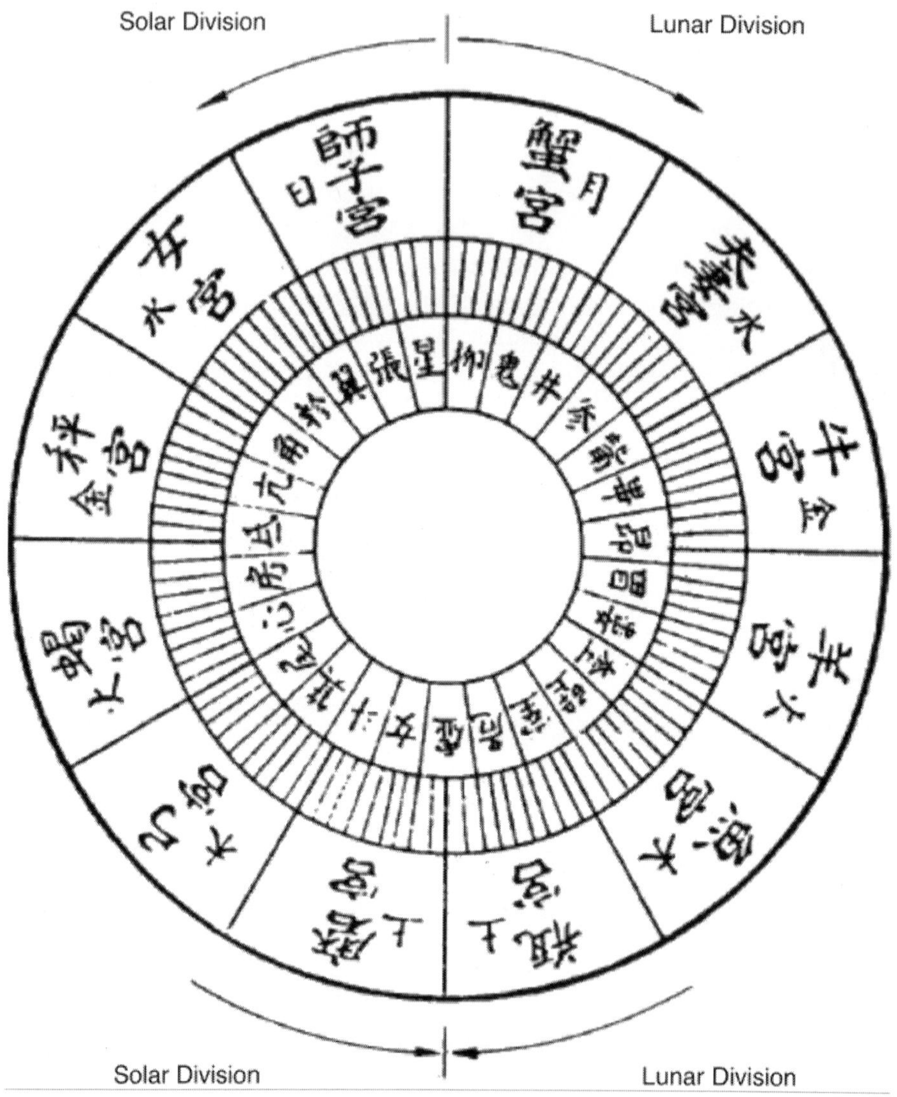

Fig.25 Correspondence between the twelve zodiacal signs and the twenty-seven *nakṣatra*-s with planetary assignment.

The idea of arranging the twelve zodiacal signs as houses for the seven luminaries originated in Greece. The idea presented here is described in Ptolemy's *Tetrabiblos* I.17. The system spread quickly to India (*Yavanajātaka* 1.32–33) after its development in the Mediterranean world. Establishing the correspondence between the twelve zodiacal signs and the twenty-seven *nakṣatra*-s was the first step to adapt Greek astrology to the Indian system. The beginning of the extant manuscript of the *Yavanajātaka* has been lost. This missing part is very likely to have mentioned the relation between the zodiacal signs and the *nakṣatra*-s. Evidence for this may be the fragmentary citations of the missing verses found in the later commentaries.

Zodiacal sign	Domain	Character and fortune
Leo	Career, wealth	Lively, materially abundant, pious to one's parents. Control armies.
Virgo	Wife, concubines, love affairs	Hidden feelings. Many children both male and female. Endowed with wealth. Hold duties in palace.
Libra	Treasure	Gentle and quiet. Religious, reverent and wealthy. Tendency to control financial matters.
Scorpio	Sickness	Sickly. Envious. Occupied in medical field.
Sagittarius	Joy, celebration	Like to plan. Take up post as generals or ministers.
Capricorn	Fight	Rebellious. Neglect one's wife. Occupied in duties related to execution.
Aquarius	Victory, strength	Confident, learned and rich. Occupied in scholarly field.
Pisces	Career, duties	Invincible if one becomes general or minister. Learned, reliable. Occupied in works related to compilation of historical texts.
Aries	Social affairs	Good fortune. Healthy, long-lived and tenacious. Occupied in culinary field.
Taurus	Animal, husbandry	Occupied in husbandry.
Gemini	Progeny	Many wives. Loved by many. Occupied in works related to treasury (*huyu* 戶鑰).
Cancer	Quarrel, court affairs	Vicious and like to cheat others. Intelligent. Short-lived. Occupied in judicial field.

Fig.26 Domain, character and fortune of the twelve zodiacal signs.

The relation between the zodiacal signs and the *nakṣatra*-s was versified by different Indian scholars of later times and became popular knowledge. A verse such as this is memorized by many modern Indians even today:

> Aries consists of *Aśvinī*, *Bharaṇī* and a quarter of *Kṛttikā*,
> Taurus consists of three quarters of *Kṛttikā*, *Rohiṇī* and half of *Mṛgaśīrṣa*.[28]

Amoghavajra too might have heard something similar from his Brahmin uncle or when he was travelling in South India. In the *Xiuyao jing* based on his teaching, Amoghavajra described the domain of influence each zodiacal sign had over the human world, the general character and the typical occupations of people belonging to each zodiacal sign (although he did not define what it means to belong to a sign).

Size of the Seven Luminaries

The text gives the size of each of the seven luminaries. This is a curious topic that deserves closer examination. The size is described as "width," which probably refers to the diameter.

Sun	51 yojanas
Moon	50 yojanas
Venus	10 yojanas
Jupiter	9 yojanas
Mercury	8 yojanas
Mars	7 yojanas
Saturn	6 yojanas

The unit of length, *youxun* 由旬, used in the Chinese text is the transliteration of the Sanskrit *yojana*. The precise value of the unit is unclear as weights and measures were not standardized in ancient India. In the astronomical work *Āryabhaṭīya*, one *yojana* is said to be eight thousand times of the height of a man. The diameter of the seven luminaries together with the earth according to *Āryabhaṭīya* are as follows (units in *yojana*):

[28] *aśvinyo 'tha bharaṇyo bahulāpādaś ca kīrtyate meṣaḥ | vṛṣabho bahulāśeṣaṃ rohiṇyo 'rdhaṃ ca mṛgaśirasaḥ* ||… *Bṛhatsaṃhitā* 101.1–6.

Earth	1050.0
Sun	4410.0
Moon	315.0
Venus	63.0
Jupiter	31.5
Mercury	21.0
Saturn	15.75
Mars	12.6

What is interesting is that the widths of the Sun and the Moon described in the *Xiuyao jing* are the same as those described in the *Abhidharmakośabhāṣya* in both Chinese translation and the extant Sanskrit recension. In the *Xiuyao jing*, the lines that follow appear to be quoted from the *Abhidharmakośabhāṣya*, revealing Amoghavajra's Buddhist background.

In the second half of the first chapter of the *Xiuyao jing*, a passage begins with the following remark:

> For the Indian month, the first day [up to the fifteenth day] is called the bright *pakṣa* and the sixteenth day [up to the thirtieth day] is called the dark *pakṣa*. In the Primordial Past, in the bright *pakṣa*, on the new moon day of the second month, which was [also] the spring equinox, when the luminaries were aligned at the lodge Lou [= Aśvinī], and the Sun was crossing the equator from south to north according to the gnomon, the weather was warm, all living things prospered and everything grew. Brahmā rejoiced and declared [this day] to be the Epoch.
>
> 天竺月名一日為白博叉，十六日為黑博叉。上古白博叉，二月春分朔，于時曜躔婁宿，道[29]齊景正。日中氣和、庶物漸榮，一切增長。梵天歡喜。命為歲元。

This is apparently a note added by Yang Jingfeng when he revised the translation. The underlined part is in fact quoted from another text known as the *Jiuzhi li* 九執曆, a work of astronomical calculation composed by the Indian astronomer Gautamasiddha 瞿曇悉達 in 718 CE. The fact that Yang Jingfeng was conversant with this work is apparent in the subsequent section of the text, entitled *Suanyaozhi zhang* 算曜直章.

[29] T 21.388a.

Bright and Dark Half-Months

The passage quoted above is an explanation of the Epoch (that is, starting date for calculation) of the Indian calendar. First, it is described that in India, a month—that is from one new moon to the next new moon or alternatively from one full moon to the next—is divided into two half-months, known as *śukla-pakṣa*, or the "bright half-month," and *kṛṣṇa-pakṣa*, or the "dark half-month." The starting point of the Epoch is identified as the vernal equinox that coincides with the first day of the white half-month of *Caitra*, corresponding to the second month in China. To be precise, this is the day when both the Sun and the Moon are located at the first degree of *Aśvinī*, which can be assumed to be the spring equinox. This contrasts with the Chinese system in which the Epoch is chosen based on the agreement of the following parameters: the eleventh month, the first day of the sexagesimal cycle (*jiazi* 甲子), the conjunction of Sun and Moon, midnight (*dan* 旦) and the winter solstice (Yabuuti 1980:112).

Indian and Chinese Names of the Months

Yang Jingfeng gives the corresponding Indian and Chinese names of the months:

Indian month (in Sanskrit and Chinese)	Chinese month
Caitra 角月	second
Vaiśākha 氐月	third
Jyaiṣṭha 心月	fourth
Āṣāḍha 箕月	fifth
Śrāvaṇa 女月	sixth
Bhādrapada 室月	seventh
Āśvina 婁月	eighth
Kārttika 昴月	ninth
Mārgaśira 觜月	tenth
Pauṣa 鬼月	eleventh
Māgha 星月	twelfth
Phālguna 翼月	first

If one compares the Sanskrit names of the months to the names of the *nakṣatra*-s as found on p.50, one can see that the former is derived from the latter. This is described also in Shi Yao's first translation, or the second fascicle of the *Xiuyao jing*, where it is said, "In India (lit. the Western Land) one calls the month by the name of the *nakṣatra* of the fifteenth day." In other words, the name of the *nakṣatra* where the Moon is located in the full moon night is used as the name for that month. For example, at the time of spring equinox, the Sun is in *Aśvinī* (the lodge *Lou*), and the Moon on the full moon day would be in *Citrā* (the lodge *Jiao*), 180° away. Therefore, the month is called Caitra (derived from *Citrā*).

Correspondence between *Nakṣatra*-s and Days

Next in the text is the *Yuexiu bangtong li* 月宿傍通暦, or "Moon-*Nakṣatra* Correspondence Table," which gives the correspondence between the *nakṣatra*-s and the days. The table found in the Japanese manuscripts is different from the one in the Continental edition—the former adopts the twenty-seven *nakṣatra* system while the latter is based on the twenty-eight *nakṣatra* system. With regard to the question of which of the two is closer to what Amoghavajra transmitted, I favor the former. That is because even apart from this example, the twenty-seven *nakṣatra*-s appear frequently in the first fascicle of the Japanese edition. Furthermore, with the exception of only one instance, the twenty-seven *nakṣatra* system is used throughout the second fascicle, which is thought to be closer to the not yet Sinicized original. While a system of twenty-eight *nakṣatra*-s also appears in Indian astrology, and both systems appear in the Chinese translations of the *Śārdūlakarṇāvadāna* (*Modengjia jing* 摩登伽經 and *Shetoujian taizi ershibaxiu jing* 舍頭諫太子二十八宿經), the text that Amoghavajra transmitted primarily employs the twenty-seven *nakṣatra* system. It was Yang Jingfeng, the Chinese editor, who altered the text of the *Xiuyao jing* at various occasions to make the *nakṣatra*-s twenty-eight. The sinicization of the text continued even after Yang Jingfeng to become the Continental edition we know today.

On the other hand, the *Xiuyao jing* as brought to Japan by Kūkai retains its original form and was preserved and transmitted as such for a long time. This twenty-seven *nakṣatra* system continued to be used in the *Senmyōreki* 宣明暦 (862–1684 CE), replaced only during the Edo Period (in the reformatory 1684 *Jōkyōreki* 貞享暦) by the twenty-eight *nakṣatra* system popular in China.[30]

[30] Watanabe 1976:82.

How then should the twenty-seven *nakṣatra*-s be assigned to the days? In the first fascicle of the *Xiuyao jing*, a table is provided to clarify the matter; in the second fascicle, instead of a table, a written explanation is given. The latter is furnished with further details in the Continental edition. According to the table, one first finds out which *nakṣatra* the Moon is in on the full moon day of a particular month. If the particular day one has in mind is before the fifteenth, one counts backward by one *nakṣatra* per day; if it is after the fifteenth, one counts forward.

In other words, in a simplified manner, a month is divided into thirty days, each corresponding to a *nakṣatra*. From the full moon day of each month, counting a maximum of fifteen *nakṣatra*-s should not result in much discrepancy. While the *nakṣatra* of the full moon day of every lunation is not fixed each year, in the first fascicle of the Japanese edition of the *Xiuyao jing*, the twelve *nakṣatra*-s used for the names of each month are chosen and assigned as the *nakṣatra* of the fifteenth day of the corresponding month. This serves as the basis of the *Yuexiu bangtong li*, presented here as Fig.27. This table is therefore artificial and idealized, making all months thirty days and with no consideration for intercalation.

The Continental edition simply assigns a *nakṣatra* to each day, disregarding any actual observation. The twenty-eight *nakṣatra*-s, that is, with *Abhijit* or the lodge *Niu* 牛 added to the twenty-seven *nakṣatra*-s, are assigned consecutively to the three hundred sixty days in the table. This results in a gap of four *nakṣatra*-s between *Mūla* (or *Wei* 尾) at the end of one year (thirtieth day of the twelfth month) and *Dhaniṣṭhā* (or *Xu* 虛) at the beginning of the next (first day of the first month). Needless to say, such tabulation is astronomically meaningless.

According to Watanabe, in the Japanese calendar *Senmyōreki* 宣明暦,[32] the *nakṣatra* of the new moon day (first day) of each month is made the *nakṣatra* of that month. Then, from that day, the twenty-seven *nakṣatra*-s are assigned to the remaining days of the month.[33] The *nakṣatra*-s of the new moon days in the *Senmyōreki* are in fact identical to those in the table of the first fascicle of the Japanese manuscript of the *Xiuyao jing*. Furthermore, a different table was prepared for the intercalary month in the *Senmyōreki*.

---

[32] Translator's note: This is a Chinese Tang-dynasty calendar system adopted in Japan from 861–1684 CE.

[33] Watanabe 1976:83.

d / m	1	2	3	4	5	6	7	8	9	10	11	12	13	14	15	16	17	18	19	20	21	22	23	24	25	26	27	28	29	30
2nd	奎	婁	胃	昴	畢	觜	參	井	鬼	柳	星	張	翼	軫	角	亢	氐	房	心	尾	箕	斗	女	虛	危	室	壁	奎	婁	胃
3rd	胃	昴	畢	觜	參	井	鬼	柳	星	張	翼	軫	角	亢	氐	房	心	尾	箕	斗	女	虛	危	室	壁	奎	婁	胃	昴	畢
4th	畢	觜	參	井	鬼	柳	星	張	翼	軫	角	亢	氐	房	心	尾	箕	斗	女	虛	危	室	壁	奎	婁	胃	昴	畢	觜	參
5th	參	井	鬼	柳	星	張	翼	軫	角	亢	氐	房	心	尾	箕	斗	女	虛	危	室	壁	奎	婁	胃	昴	畢	觜	參	井	鬼
6th	鬼	柳	星	張	翼	軫	角	亢	氐	房	心	尾	箕	斗	女	虛	危	室	壁	奎	婁	胃	昴	畢	觜	參	井	鬼	柳	星
7th	張	翼	軫	角	亢	氐	房	心	尾	箕	斗	女	虛	危	室	壁	奎	婁	胃	昴	畢	觜	參	井	鬼	柳	星	張	翼	軫
8th	角	亢	氐	房	心	尾	箕	斗	女	虛	危	室	壁	奎	婁	胃	昴	畢	觜	參	井	鬼	柳	星	張	翼	軫	角	亢	氐
9th	氐	房	心	尾	箕	斗	女	虛	危	室	壁	奎	婁	胃	昴	畢	觜	參	井	鬼	柳	星	張	翼	軫	角	亢	氐	房	心
10th	心	尾	箕	斗	女	虛	危	室	壁	奎	婁	胃	昴	畢	觜	參	井	鬼	柳	星	張	翼	軫	角	亢	氐	房	心	尾	箕
11th	斗	女	虛	危	室	壁	奎	婁	胃	昴	畢	觜	參	井	鬼	柳	星	張	翼	軫	角	亢	氐	房	心	尾	箕	斗	女	虛
12th	虛	危	室	壁	奎	婁	胃	昴	畢	觜	參	井	鬼	柳	星	張	翼	軫	角	亢	氐	房	心	尾	箕	斗	女	虛	危	室
1st	室	壁	奎	婁	胃	昴	畢	觜	參	井	鬼	柳	星	張	翼	軫	角	亢	氐	房	心	尾	箕	斗	女	虛	危	室	壁	奎

Fig.27 Moon-*Nakṣatra* Correspondence Table Based on the Kakushō Edition.[31]

[31] m = month, d = day. The tabulation is based on the Kakushō edition, which is completely different from the Continental edition. Beside the difference of twenty-seven vs. twenty-eight mansions, there are also other indiciations which suggest that the latter had undergone considerable sinicization. The table in the Kakushō edition begins with the Chinese second month, which corresponds to the Indian month of *Caitra*, the new moon of which is considered the beginning of the Indian calendar year according to the *amānta* (new-moon ending) system. The one in the Continental edition does not take moon phases into consideration.

Incidentally, curious about how this appears in almanacs in modern Japan and looking at a nearby copy of the 1986 *Kōfukureki* 幸福暦,[34] the author noted to his surprise that the *nakṣatra*-s of the fifteenth day of each month in the old calendar is the same as those in the Japanese manuscript of the *Xiuyao jing*. There are remarks here and there in the almanac saying that "the twenty-eight *nakṣatra*-s of this work are arranged according to the *old method* (i.e., twenty-seven *nakṣatra*-s), and the lunar lodge *Niu* (*Abhijit*) is not assigned." While the method in this calendar may be considered a revival of the *Xiuyao jing*, such method is not yet well recognized today. For instance, the calendar that the author received from a nearby bank, as well as the one issued by the Kurama Temple in Kyoto, are based on the twenty-eight *nakṣatra* system.

Since the assignment of twenty-seven or twenty-eight *nakṣatra*-s varies depending on the almanac, people can become confused even today. In a newspaper column called "*Hai! Shakaibu desu*" in the *Asahi Shimbun*, dated 29th January, 1986 (Osaka edition), a housewife from Osaka asked:

> "I have got hold of copies of almanacs from different Shinto Shrines and bookstores and I have been using them... Recently, I have become interested in the 'twenty-eight *nakṣatra*-s," which indicate the auspiciousness of each day. However, when I compare the four almanacs I have in my possession, I notice that different *nakṣatra*-s are assigned to the same day. After checking it seems to me that there might be two systems of "twenty-eight *nakṣatra*-s." Could one of them be wrong?"

In response, Enomoto Shoten (Osaka), one of the publishers of the almanacs, gave the following answer:

> "You should consider the twenty-eight *nakṣatra*-s as constellations that indicate the daily position of the Moon. In India, where this system originated, there were twenty-seven *nakṣatra*-s; however, a method with twenty-eight *nakṣatra*-s arose in China. Both systems were transmitted to Japan. In the case of the twenty-seven *nakṣatra* system, the first day of each month in the old calendar system is adjusted to match the phases of the Moon. As a result, sometimes a *nakṣatra* in sequence may be skipped, while in other time the same *nakṣatra* may be applied to two consecutive days. We have used this method for our calendar. The other method lines up the twenty-eight *nakṣatra*-s in order

[34] Published by Enomoto Shoten 榎本書店, compiled by Takashima Ekidan Honbu 高島易断本部.

> without considering the actual lunar movement. Even nowadays, almanac editors have adopted the two different systems based on various considerations. The users should therefore decide for themselves which system they want to believe in."

In my opinion, it is better not to believe in something which the users are left to decide for themselves. Nonetheless, since divination is in general harmless—as the Japanese idiom goes, "Saved are those who believe"—to tell the faithful not to believe may perhaps be insensitive. I cannot help but express my wonder at the fact that Indian astrology survives to this day in Japan after so many centuries and is even being revived.

After explaining the mathematical nature of the twenty-seven *nakṣatra*-s and the artificial Moon-*nakṣatra* correspondence, as a supplementary remark toward the end of the first chapter, the text of the *Xiuyao jing* introduces the idea that the Moon's daily position could be ahead or behind the actual observed position due to the uneven longitudinal width of the twenty-seven *nakṣatra*-s or asterisms. This explanation is summarized at the end in a verse. Since the verse is found in practically the same form in the second fascicle as well, it is quoted below.

> 六宿未到名合月　十二宿月左右合
> 九宿如犢隨母行　從奎宿數應當知
>
> Six *nakṣatra*-s are said to have been in conjunction with the Moon although [the Moon] has not yet arrived. Twelve *nakṣatra*-s form a conjunction more or less with the Moon.
>
> Nine *nakṣatra*-s move like calves following their mother. One should know that one counts from *Kui* (*Revātī*).

In other words, the six *nakṣatra*-s from *Kui* 奎 (27. *Revati*) to *Zui* 觜 (5. *Mṛgaśīrṣa*) are said to have been in conjunction with the Moon even though the Moon has not actually reached them; the twelve *nakṣatra*-s from *Shen* 參 (6. *Ārdrā*) to *Fang* 房 (17. *Anurādhā*) align exactly with the Moon; and the nine *nakṣatra*-s from *Xin* 心 (18. *Jyseṣṭhā*) to *Bi* 壁 (26. *Uttarabhādrapadā*) are said to be like the calves following a cow, trailing behind the Moon. Such a threefold categorization of *nakṣatra*-s based on their relationship with the Moon appears to have originated in ancient times, as it is also found in the *Śārdūlakarṇāvadāna* and its two Chinese translations, the *Atharvavedapariśiṣṭa*, as well as in the *Bṛhatsaṃhitā*. In particular, in the *Śārdūlakarṇāvadāna* the same analogy of cow and calves is used.

2. The Twenty-eight *Nakṣatra*-s

The purpose of the second chapter of the *Xiuyao jing* is to give a detailed description of each of the twenty-eight *nakṣatra*-s. The material corresponding to this chapter appears also in the second fascicle of the text under the title "Calendar of Auspiciousness and Inauspiciousness Resulting from the Twenty-Seven *Nakṣatra*-s" 二十七宿所為吉凶暦, where the twenty-seven *nakṣatra*-s are discussed, with the exception of *Niu* 牛 (*abhijit*). In the first fascicle of the Japanese edition, *Niu* is not placed in its original position between *Dou* 斗 and *Nü* 女 but is placed after *Wei* 胃 as the final *nakṣatra* or lodge. It must be Yang Jingfeng who made this change, with or without Amoghavajra's approval. In the Continental edition, this positioning was further modified and *Niu* was placed in between *Dou* and *Nü*. We shall return to the problem of *Niu* later.

Beginning of the Twenty-eight *Nakṣatra*-s

Here one should first note that in both the first and second fascicles, the description of the twenty-eight (or twenty-seven) *nakṣatra*-s begins with *Mao* 昴 (*Kṛttikā*). In Fig.23 on p.50, *Lou* 婁 (*Aśvinī*) was assigned the first *nakṣatra*. The reason for this is that in Greco-Indian astronomy and astrology, the beginning of Aries (= *meṣādi*, 0°) is taken as the starting point of the ecliptic coordinates, which the Indian astronomers considered as equivalent to the beginning of *Aśvinī* (*aśvinyādi* = beginning of *Lou* 婁, 0°). This becomes apparent if one looks at Fig.24 as explained in the first chapter of *Xiuyao jing*.

In earlier periods, it was customary to count the *nakṣatra*-s from *Mao* 昴 (*Kṛttikā*). *Kṛttikā* refers to the star cluster Pleiades of the constellation Taurus, or its main star η Tauri. As such, one would like to imagine that when the twenty-eight (or twenty-seven) *nakṣatra* system starting from *Kṛttikā* came into existence, the vernal equinox must have been close to η Tauri. As we have discussed concerning the phenomenon of precession (the retrograde movement of the vernal equinox) on pp.28, 33, it is known that η Tauri was close to the vernal

Fig.28 Indus Valley Scripts.
(http://upload.wikimedia.org/wikipedia/commons/3/32/IndusValleySeals.JPG)

equinox at around 2300 BCE. One might thus conclude that the *nakṣatra* system came into existence in India at that time.

In fact, many Indians advocate such a view and not a few scholars claim that "Indian astronomy is very old." However, the *nakṣatra*-s as lunar mansions are not mentioned in the *Ṛg-veda*, India's oldest text, which is dated to as early as 1500 BCE. In 2300 BCE, the Aryans had yet to arrive on the Indian subcontinent. This was an era when a non-Aryan civilization called the "Indus civilization" flourished. As the seal script used by the people of this civilization has not been yet deciphered, there is little one can say about the nature of astronomy in it. Nonetheless, to take a contrary approach, some scholars have tried to decipher the script based on the assumptions that some of the undeciphered characters are connected with the *nakṣatra*-s.

Among ancient civilizations, the twenty-seven (or twenty-eight) *nakṣatra*-s were known only in China and India; they are not mentioned, for example, in cuneiform texts. Therefore, it may not be completely preposterous to suggest that such knowledge was possessed by the inhabitants of India prior to the arrival of the Aryans. However, it is difficult to prove this through philological methods. Among Chinese scholars there are those who claim that the twenty-eight lunar lodges were transmitted to India to become the *nakṣatra*-s; the proofs are however rather weak. As a case in point, the stars actually shared by the Chinese and Indian systems are too few in number to support such a hypothesis.

Number of Stars, Shape and Presiding Deity of Each *Nakṣatra*

In the second chapter of the *Xiuyao jing*, the following eight items are described for each *nakṣatra*:

1. Number of stars comprising the *nakṣatra*
2. Shape of the *nakṣatra*
3. Presiding deity of the *nakṣatra*
4. Clan (*gotra*) to which the *nakṣatra* belongs
5. Food offered to the corresponding deity on the day when the Moon is positioned in the *nakṣatra*
6. Prescribed and proscribed activities for each *nakṣatra* day, when the Moon is positioned in the *nakṣatra*
7. Whether it would be auspicious to make clothes on that day
8. Character and fortune of the person born under the *nakṣatra*

The items in the above list, excepting no.7, are found also in the *Śārdūlakarṇāvadāna* and its two Chinese translations. Furthermore, in the *Pariśiṣṭa* of the *Atharvaveda* there are several similar records. While a comparative examination of each list item for every *nakṣatra* may yield some interesting results, I have summarized here only the first three items from the first fascicle of the *Xiuyao jing*, together with some additional remarks.

I. *Mao* 昴 (*Kṛttikā*)

1. Six stars (The Pleiades—main star is η Tauri).
2. Razor—due to the false analysis that the word *kṛttikā* was derived from the verb *kṛt* ("cut").
3. *Agni*—translated as "Fire God" (*Huosen* 火神).

II. *Bi* 畢 (*Rohiṇī*)

1. Five stars (α, θ, γ, δ, ε Tauri. α Tauri is also known as Aldebaran).
2. Chariot—it resembles the shape of a chariot as it was called Rohiṇī's chariot (*rohiṇīśakaṭa*).
3. *Prajāpati*—translated as the deity of *Boshebodi* 鉢闍鉢底.

III. *Zui* 觜 (*Mṛgaśīrṣa*)

1. Three stars (λ, ϕ_1, ϕ_2 Orionis).
2. Deer head—the name "head (*śīrṣa*) of a deer (*mṛga*)" was thought to indicate its shape.
3. *Soma*—translated as "Moon God" (*Yueshen* 月神).

IV. *Shen* 參 (*Ārdrā*)

1. One star (α Orionis). The Chinese name *shen* originates from the three stars of the belt of Orion.
2. Dot on the forehead—The dot (*tilaka*) put on the forehead of Indians. The *Modengjia jing* makes the shape of all *nakṣatra*-s consisting of only one star a "head jewel" (*dingzhu* 頂珠).
3. *Rudra*—translated as the deity of *Ludaluo* 魯達羅.

V. *Jing* 井 (*Punarvasū*)

1. Two stars (α, β Gemini).
2. "Wufu" 屋栿 (?)[35]—In the *Modengjia jing*, all *nakṣatra*-s of two stars are made "human steps" (*renbu* 人步).
3. Sun God (*rishen* 日神)—*Aditi* should be the presiding god of this *nakṣatra*. It appears that it was mistaken as the Sun (*Āditya*), the son of *Aditi*.

VI. *Gui* 鬼 (*Puṣya*)

1. Three stars (γ, δ, θ Cancri).
2. Bottle—Same as in the *Modengjia jing*. The Sanskrit gloss is *vardhamāna*, that is, a saucer in the shape of the lid of a pitcher.
3. *Bṛhaspati*—translated as the deity of *Bilihesabodi* 蘖利訶駁撥底.

VII. *Liu* 柳 (*Āśleṣā*)

1. Six stars (δ, ε, η, ρ, σ, ζ Hydrae).
2. Snake head—The Sanskrit name means "entwined." While the image of a snake is the same as the one in the West, the six stars in the Indian *nakṣatra* depict only the head of the hydra.
3. *Śeṣa*—In all texts and editions, the Chinese characters *Bishe* 毗舍 are given. I have corrected it to *Cishe* 眦舍, which is closer to *śeṣa*, one of the words meaning snake in Sanskrit.

VIII. *Xing* 星 (*Maghā*)

1. Six stars (α, η, γ, ζ, μ, ε Leonis)

[35] Translator's note: "Crossbeam of house."

2. *Qiang* 牆 ("Wall")—*Maghā* means prosperity and wealth; *Qiang* is "boundary." It was made *Hequ* 河曲 in the old texts.
3. *Bhaga*—translated as the deity *Bojia* 薄伽神. It was translated as "Ghost God" (*guishen* 鬼神) in the *Modengjia jing* and "Father Deity" (*futian* 父天) in the *Shetoujian jing*. These correspond to *pitara*-s, the ancestor spirits in India. *Bhaga* should be the presiding deity for the next *nakṣatra Zhang* 張 (*Pūrvaphalgunī*).

IX. *Zhang* 張 (*Pūrvaphalgunī*)

1. Six stars—Referred to usually as two stars (δ, θ Leonis); it has six stars in the *Xiuyao jing*.
2. Chu 杵[36]—"Human steps" (*Renbu* 人步) in the *Modengjia jing*.
3. *Vasu*—translated as the deity of *Posou* 婆藪神, the auspicious god, *Shanshen* 善神, in the *Modengjia jing* and *Shantian* 善天 in the *Shetoujian jing*. Both should be the translations of the Sanskrit *bhaga*. It is not clear why it has become Vasu here. See also *Xu* 虛 (XXI).

X. *Yi* 翼 (*Uttaraphalgunī*)

1. Two stars (β, 93 Leonis)
2. Jiafu 跏趺—Sitting cross-legged in the lotus position.
3. *Aryamā*—translated as the deity "Liyemo" 利耶摩神 (with the first syllable dropped). There are cases when the presiding deities of the *Pūrvaphalgunī* (*Zhang*) and *Uttaraphalgunī* (*Yi*) are interchanged with each other.

XI. *Zhen* 軫 (*Hasta*)

1. Five stars (δ, γ, ε, α, β Corvii)
2. Hand—Literally what *hasta* means. The above five stars may have been thought to be in the shape of an outstretched palm.
3. Savitṛ—translated as *Suobitanli* 娑毗怛利. In the text *po* 婆 was mistaken for *suo* 娑.

XII. *Jiao* 角 (*Citrā*)

1. Two stars in the *Xiuyao jing*. As all Indian texts report only one star (α Virginis)—an error in transmission is possible.
2. Changbu 長布—In the *Śārdūakarṇāvadāna*, all *nakṣatra*-s consisting of one star are described as *tilaka*.
3. Tvaṣṭṛ—translated as *Duosedieli* 埵瑟窒利.

---

[36] Translator's note: Literally, "pestle."

XIII. *Kang* 亢 (*Svāti*)

1. One star (α Bootis or Arcturus).
2. Huozhu 火珠—Fireball (?).
3. Vāyu—Wind God (*Fengshen* 風神).

XIV. Di 氐 (Viśākhā)

1. Four stars (α, β, γ, ι Librae).
2. Horn or cow horn.
3. Indrāgnī—translated as the deity of *Yintuoluoqini* 因伽陀羅祇尼.

XV. *Fang* 房 (*Anurādhā*)

1. Four stars (β, δ, π, ρ Scorpionis).
2. Changbu 長布—Or *zhuguan* 珠貫 in the *Modengjia jing*.
3. Mitra—translated as the deity of *Miduoluo* 密多羅.

XVI. *Xin* 心 (*Jyeṣṭhā*)

1. Three stars (α, σ, τ Scorpionis)
2. Jie 階[37]—Origin unknown. *mai* 麥 ("grain") in the *Shetoujian jing*, a translation of Sanskrit *yava* ("barley").
3. Indra—translated as the deity of *Yintuoluo* 因陀羅.

XVII. *Wei* 尾 (*Mūla*)

1. Nine stars (λ, υ, κ, ι, θ, η, ζ, μ, ε Scorpions)
2. Lion's mane—Similar to "lion's tail" (Skt. *siṃhapuccha*) in Indian astrological works of a relatively late period. In the *Modengjia jing*, the Chinese character *xie* 蝎 ("scorpion") is the translation of the Sanskrit *vṛścika*, whose connection with the Western counterpart is uncertain.
3. Nirṛti—translated as the deity *Nilü* 你律.

XVIII. *Ji* 箕 (*Pūrvāṣāḍhā*)

1. Four stars (γ, δ, ε, η Sagittarii)
2. Cow's steps—The four stars were probably viewed as the four feet of a cow. Same in the *Modengjia jing* and its Sanskrit version.
3. Āpas—translated as "Water God" (*Shuishen* 水神).

XVIX. *Dou* 斗 (*Uttarāṣāḍhā*)

1. Four stars (φ, σ, τ, ζ Sagittarii)
2. Elephant's steps—This is thought to resemble the elephant's steps. Same in the the *Modengjia jing*.
3. Viśva—translated as the deity of *Bishuo* 毗說神.

---

[37] Translator's note: Literally, "steps."

XX. *Nü* 女 (*Śravaṇā*)

1. Three stars (α, β, γ Aquilae. α Aquilae = Altair)
2. Plow drawn by an ox. *mai* 麥 ("grain") in the *Modengjia jing*.
3. Viṣṇu—translated as *Bisouniu* 毗藪紐.

XXI. *Xu* 虛 (*Dhaniṣṭhā*, or *Śraviṣṭhā* in earlier time)

1. Four stars (α, β, γ, δ Delphini)
2. Harītakī (name of a plant). *feiniao* 飛鳥 ("flying bird") in the *Modengjia jing*, or simply "bird" in its Sanskrit version.
3. Vasavaḥ—plural of *Vasu*, translated as the deity *Posuo* 婆娑神. See also *Pūrvaphalgunī* (IX).

XXII. *Wei* 危 (*Śatabhiṣaj*)

1. Hundred stars—The reading "hundred stars" in the Japanese edition of the *Xiuyao jing* is interesting as the Sanskrit name itself means literally "having a hundred physicians." In the *Shetoujian jing*, it was translated as *Baidu xiu* 百毒宿.[38] In the old texts, the *nakṣatra* refers to the single star λ Aquarii. However, from its name it is natural to associate it with a hundred stars as Varāhamihira did.[39]
2. *Huasui* 花穗—"Flowers" (?).
3. Varuṇa—translated as the deity of *Polunu* 婆魯拏神.

XXIII. *Shi* 室 (*Pūrvabhādrapadā*)

1. Two stars (α, β Pegasi).
2. Thill (shaft attached to a cart).
3. Ajapāda—translated as the deity of *Axibutuo* 阿醯布陀.

XXIV. *Bi* 壁 (*Uttarabhādrapadā*)

1. Two stars (γ Pegasi and α Andromedae).
2. Standing pole.
3. Ahirbudhnya—translated as the deity *Nituoluo* 尼陀羅.[40]

XXV. *Kui* 奎 (*Revatī*)

1. Thirty-two stars—In the old texts such as the *Modengjia jing*, it refers to one star, ζ Piscium. Later, it appears that the neighboring stars were included as well.

---

[38] Translator's note: Literally, "the lodge of the hundred poisons."

[39] At the beginning of the chapter titled "Nakṣatrakarmaguṇādhyāya" (*Bṛhatsaṃhitā* 97.1–2), the number of stars for the twenty-seven *nakṣatra*-s is given. The twenty-fourth *nakṣatra* counting from *Aśvinī*, namely *Śatabhiṣaj*, is said to contain a hundred (*śata*) stars.

[40] Translator's note: Possibly a transliteration of *nidrā*.

2. Small boat.
3. Pūṣā—translated as the deity of *Bushe* 逋涉.

XXVI. *Lou* 婁 (*Aśvinī*, or in earlier time, *Aśvayujau*)

1. In the older period, it usually refers to the two stars (β, γ Arietis); in the *Xiuyao jing*, it refers to "three stars."
2. Horse Head (*Matou* 馬頭)—same in the *Modengjia jing* (*Mashou* 馬首). Both come from *Aśvayujau*, meaning "something which ties the horse".
3. Gandharva—translated as the deity of *Qianda* 乾闥. The name appears also in the Sanskrit *Śārdūlakarṇāvadāna*. The presiding deity is omitted in the *Modengjia jing*; in the *Shetoujian jing*, it becomes *Xiangshen* 香神 ("Fragrant God"). The latter is an interpretation whereby *gandharva* connects to *gandha* ("fragrance"). Incidentally, in the *Atharvavedapariśiṣṭa*, the twin-gods Aśvins (*Aśvinau*), whose name is identical to this *nakṣatra*, become the presiding deities.

XXVII. *Wei* 胃 (*Bharaṇī*)

1. Three stars (35, 39, 41 Arietis).
2. Triangle—*dingzu* 鼎足 in the *Modengjia jing* and *ke* 軻 in the *Shetoujian jing*. In the Sanskrit text, it is *bhaga* (female reproductive organ).
3. Yama—translated as the deity of *Yanmo* 閻摩神.

XXVIII. *Niu* 牛 (*Abhijit*)

While *Niu* is listed as the twenty-eighth mansion in the Japanese edition of the *Xiuyao jing*, it should have been placed between *Dou*, the nineteenth lodge, and *Nü*, the twentieth lodge, whenever twenty-eight *nakṣatra*-s are listed, as is the case in the Continental versions. However, as discussed earlier, the Japanese edition should be considered closer to the original.

1. Three stars (α, ε, ζ Lyrae)—the star α is also known as Vega (the lady weaver or *Zhinü* 織女 in Chinese). All twenty-seven other *nakṣatra*-s are located close to either the ecliptic or the equator; only this *nakṣatra* is located more than 60° north of the ecliptic. It is therefore inappropriate to consider *Niu* a "lunar lodge." The justification for the presence of this *nakṣatra* concerns the question of the origin of the twenty-eight *nakṣatra*-s, which has been debated among Western scholars since the nineteenth

century.[41] At any rate, as far as Indian literature is concerned, *Abhijit* is often not given the same status as the other *nakṣatra*-s. In the modern time, the system of twenty-seven *nakṣatra*-s—that is, excluding *Abhijit*—is used in Indian astrology.

2. Ox Head—The description of the shape "Ox's Head" (*gośīrṣa*) is found in the Sanskrit *Śārdūlakarṇāvadāna*. This description is unrelated to the Chinese lodge *Niu* (lit. "ox"/"cow"), which in fact points to a totally different star, β Capricorni.
3. Brahmā—translated as the deity *Fanmo* 梵摩神.

As described above, the twenty-seven (or twenty-eight) *nakṣatra* system of the second chapter of the *Xiuyao jing* is completely different from that of the first chapter. Instead of being based on ecliptic coordinates of equal length, they represent the older Indian *nakṣatra*-s. The reason why I have included here the number of constituent stars and the name of the *nakṣatra*-s following each Sanskrit name is to show that in many cases the Chinese names are supplied as a matter of convenience, and the Indian *nakṣatra*-s and the Chinese "lodges" refer actually to different stars. Without keeping this in mind, one would readily confuse the two systems, thinking that they are the same. To take one example, the Indian *Abhijit* is translated as *Niu* 牛 in Chinese. Its main star is Vega (α Lyr), equivalent to the Chinese star *Zhinü* 織女; on the other hand, *Śravaṇā* was translated as *Nü* 女 in Chinese, whose main star among the three constituent stars is Altair (α Aql), or in Chinese, *Qianniu* 牽牛. In the Chinese system, the representative stars (*juxing* 距星, i.e., "standard star") of the Chinese lodges *Niu* 牛 and *Nü* 女 in fact are different stars (*β* Cap and *ε* Aqr respectively).

In Chinese astronomy, the standard stars of each lunar lodge are determined and the number of degrees separating the standard stars is called the "lodge degree" (*xiudu* 宿度). Similarly, in Indian astronomy, the standard stars are called *yogatārā* (i.e., "junction stars"), and there are texts that give their positions. Unfortunately, it is not easy to ascertain the actual stars to which they refer. In the *Brāhmasphuṭasiddhānta*,[42] a work by Brahmagupta dated to 628 CE, and one of the oldest works in which such a list is found, only seven junction stars match the Chinese standard stars.

---

[41] Yano 2011:125–32.

[42] *Brahmasphuṭasiddhānta* Ch.10.

Despite such discrepancies, the Indian *nakṣatra*-s and the twenty-eight Chinese lodges appear to have gradually merged together. In Japan, where India could only be known through China, such confusion was commonplace.

Fig.29 "Fire God" (*Butsuzōzui* 仏像図彙)

Fig.30 "Earth God" (*Butsuzōzui* 仏像図彙)

Fig.31 "Sun God" (*Butsuzōzui* 仏像図彙)

The Categorization of the Twenty-seven *Nakṣatra*-s

At the end of the second chapter of the first fascicle of the *Xiuyao jing*, the twenty-seven *nakṣatra*-s are categorized into the following seven groups:[43]

i) Peaceful and steady *nakṣatra*-s: *Bi* 畢, *Yi* 翼, *Dou* 斗, *Bi* 壁	[*dhruva*]—steady, unmovable
ii) Gentle and kind *nakṣatra*-s: *Zui* 觜, *Jiao* 角, *Fang* 房, *Kui* 奎	[*mṛdu*]—soft
iii) Poisonous and harmful *nakṣatra*-s: *Shen* 參, *Liu* 柳, *Xin* 心, *Wei* 尾	[*tīkṣṇa*]—violent
iv) Fast-moving *nakṣatra*-s: *Gui* 鬼, *Zhen* 軫, *Wei* 胃, *Lou* 婁	[*laghu*]— light
v) Fierce and mean *nakṣatra*-s: *Xing* 星, *Zhang* 張, *Ji* 箕, *Shi* 室	[*ugra*]—fearsome
vi) Light and speedy *nakṣatra*-s: *Jing* 井, *Kang* 亢, *Nü* 女, *Xu* 虚, *Wei* 危	[*carakarma*]—light-moving
vii) Hard and soft *nakṣatra*-s: *Mao* 昴, *Dai* 氐	[*mṛdutīkṣṇa*]—soft and violent

In the second fascicle of the *Xiuyao jing*, *Niu* is included among the "fast-moving *nakṣatra*-s" (group iv), replacing *Wei*; *Wei,* on the other hand, joins the "fierce and mean *nakṣatra*-s" (group v). While it may strike the reader as incongruous that *Niu* is found only in this part of the second fascicle, a comparison with the Indian texts suggests that the classification found in the second fascicle may be original. In Chapter 97 of Varāhamihira's *Bṛhatsaṃhitā*, *Mūla* (or *Wei*) is classified under *ugra* (group v) and *laghu* (group iv) is simply left with three *nakṣatra*-s. On the other hand, Utpala (tenth century), who commented on this passage, mentioned a system where *laghu* (group iv) contains four *nakṣatra*-s including *Mūla*, quoting from a certain Parāśara.

The division of the twenty-eight *nakṣatra*-s into categories may thus be traced back to India. In the Chinese *Modengjia jing* as well as in its Sanskrit version, the *nakṣatra*-s are classified under six categories: i) Supreme (seven mansions); ii) Fierce and mean (three mansions);

[43] The Sanskrit words supplied in the brackets [ ] are from Varāhamihira's *Bṛhatsaṃhitā*.

iii) Peaceful and kind (four mansions); iv) Soft and weak (five mansions); v) Steady (five mansions); vi) Fast-moving (four mansions). These developed eventually into the categories found in the *Bṛhatsaṃhitā* and a work by Parāśara. The Parāśara system was likely adopted first in the second fascicle of the *Xiuyao jing* and was modified in first fascicle.

Furthermore, the text describes things to be done and not to be done on each day presided over by a different *nakṣatra* (lit. *nakṣatra*-presiding day or *xiuzhiri* 宿直日), or the day when the Moon enters a *nakṣatra* based on the classification described above.

3. Categorization of the Twenty-seven *Nakṣatra*-s Based on the "Birth Nakṣatra"

According to the "Moon-*Nakṣatra* Correspondence Table" (*Yuexiu bangtong li* 月宿傍通曆, Fig.27), the *nakṣatra* a person's birthday falls on is called the "Natal *Nakṣatra*" (*mingxiu* 命宿). The tenth and the nineteenth *nakṣatra*-s from the Natal *Nakṣatra* are called the "Karma *Nakṣatra*" (*yexiu* 業宿) and the "Garbha *Nakṣatra*" (*taixiu* 胎宿), respectively. Counting off from each of these three *nakṣatra*-s, the following eight *nakṣatra*-s are called: i) Prosperity (*rong* 榮); ii) Misfortune (*shuai* 衰); iii) Peace (*an* 安); iv) Danger (*wei* 危); v) Success (*cheng* 成); vi) Destruction (*huai* 壞); vii) Friendship (*you* 友) and; viii) Intimacy (*qin* 親). To illustrate how this works, Yang Jingfeng gives the following example: if someone was born on the fifth day of the second month, the person would fall under *Rohinī* (*Bi* 畢) (Fig.27); *Rohinī* would be the "Birth *Nakṣatra*" (governing *nakṣatra*) of that person. Following that, the tenth *nakṣatra* counting from *Rohinī* is *Hasta* (*Zhen* 軫), which would be the "Karma *Nakṣatra*" of that person. The nineteenth *nakṣatra* is *Śravaṇā* (*Nü* 女), which would be called the "Garbha *Nakṣatra*." Thus, the corresponding *nakṣatra*-s for this particular person may be shown as Fig.32.

This method, known as the "Secret *Nakṣatra*-s of the Three Nine-s" 三九秘宿 may be described as follows: Taking the governing *nakṣatra* ("Birth *Nakṣatra*") as the starting point, first divide the twenty-seven *nakṣatra*-s into three equal parts. Let the first *nakṣatra* of the three parts be called "Life," "Karma" and "Garbha," respectively. From these three *nakṣatra*-s the following eight *nakṣatra*-s are called "Prosperity," "Decline" and so on. As such there should be eleven types of *nakṣatra*-s. In Fig.32, *Bi* 畢 is made the "Birth *Nakṣatra*" in the ring of *nakṣatra*-s. One can thus see how the correspondence between the inner and outer circles would vary depending on the person's governing *nakṣatra*.

Fig.32 Secret *Nakṣatra*-s of the Three Nine-s

The auspiciousness of these days may be deduced from their names. According to the *Xiuyao jing*:

> "Birth *Nakṣatra*" and "Garbha *Nakṣatra*"—unpropitious for undertaking any action regardless of the nature of the affair.
>
> "Karma *Nakṣatra*"—all undertakings propitious.
>
> "Prosperity *Nakṣatra*"—propitious for taking on official rank, meeting superiors, submitting a report, making offerings to the lords, trading, making clothes, wearing new clothes, and bathing. Auspicious also for monastics shaving hair, cutting nails, serving their masters, and performing rituals.

"Misfortune *Nakṣatra*," "Danger *Nakṣatra*," and "Destruction *Nakṣatra*"—bad for travel. Unpropitious also for trading, making clothes, and cutting hair and nails. However, the day of "Destruction *Nakṣatra*" is good for suppressing rebellion, conquering enemies, taking revenge and so on.

"Peace *Nakṣatra*"—good for travel, repairing one's home and household items, setting up altars and so on.

"Danger *Nakṣatra*"—good for marriage, meeting and so on.

"Success *Nakṣatra*"—propitious for study, preparation of medicines and aphrodisiacs and practice of alchemy.

"Friendship *Nakṣatra*" and "Intimacy *Nakṣatra*"—propitious for meeting friends.

In such a manner, once the individual's governing *nakṣatra* ("Birth *Nakṣatra*" or *janma-nakṣatra*) is determined, the influences of each of the twenty-seven *nakṣatra*-s has over that person can be established. This method of divination, described as the "Secret *Nakṣatra*-s of the Three-Nines" in the *Xiuyao jing*, has its origin in ancient India. Terms that could be the origin of these technical terms ("Birth," "Karma," "Prosperity" and so on) can be found in the *Bṛhadyātrā* and the Purāṇic literature:

1. 命 *ming*	*janma*—Birth
2. 業 *ye*	*karma*—Action, karma
3. 胎 *tai*	*garbhādhānaka*—Conception
4. 榮 *rong*	*sampatkara*—Bringer of prosperity
5. 衰 *shuai*	*vipatkara*—Bringer of misfortune
6. 安 *an*	*kṣema*—Peace
7. 危 *wei*	*pratyari*—Opposition
8. 成 *cheng*	*sādhaka*—Bringer of success
9. 壞 *huai*	*vaināśika*—Bringer of destruction
10. 友 *you*	*mitra*—Friendship
11. 親友 *qinyou*	*atimitra*—Intimacy

In the Sanskrit texts that I have access to, however, these technical terms are merely listed and lack further explanation. The material from the *Xiuyao jing* is thus a valuable record of how ancient Indian divination was practiced. In particular, the *Xiuyao jing* contains descriptions of situations when the *nakṣatra*-s are "occulted" (*lingfan* 凌犯, lit. "trespassed") by the seven luminaries (Sun, Moon and five planets)—namely, when the luminaries enter into the *nakṣatra*—thus bringing about harm. When an auspicious *nakṣatra* such as one belonging to the "Prosperity *Nakṣatra*-s" is interfered with by the seven luminaries, it is no longer auspicious; on the other hand, when an inauspicious *nakṣatra* such as one belonging to the "Misfortune *Nakṣatra*-s" is occulted, the inauspiciousness is removed.

Since the spatial relationship between the seven luminaries and the twenty-seven *nakṣatra*-s becomes an important matter, this topic will be discussed in the following chapter. In regard to this section, Yang Jingfeng comments:

> "Those who would like to know in which *nakṣatra*-s the Sun, Moon and the five stars are located should know that it is determined based on the Indian astronomy."

Yang then mentions the three schools of Indian astronomy that were known in China at that time. They were the Kāśyapa, the Gautama and the Kumāra. According to Yang's own words, he used Gautama's astronomical text. The astronomical text referred to here is the *Jiuzhi li* 九執曆 of Gautamasiddha (Chinese: *jutanxida* 瞿曇悉達) of the Gautama School.

Amoghavajra's *Xiuyao jing* conveys only the basics of Indian astrology and it does not teach how the planetary positions are to be calculated. Perhaps what Yang Jingfeng wanted to say is that instead of relying on Chinese astronomy right away, one should use the method of astronomical calculation transmitted from India. Unfortunately, the extant *Jiuzhi li* deals only with the positions of the Sun and the Moon and the calculation of solar and lunar eclipses, while the method of calculating planetary positions is not discussed.

4. Influences of the Seven Luminaries

The three chapters concerning the *nakṣatra*-s end here, and next the seven luminaries are discussed. First, the seven luminaries are defined as the Sun, the Moon and the five planets, after which they are described as objects shining in the sky, commanding the fate and fortune of human beings. Then the text describes how each luminary presides over a day, thus constituting a cycle of seven days. This describes precisely a method of divination that was new to China at the time when this sūtra was translated into Chinese.

In the second fascicle of the *Xiuyao jing*—namely, Shi Yao's first translation—there is a passage concerning the transmission of the days of the week, which is interesting from a historical perspective, as noted by Western scholars long ago. Among the better-known articles on the subject is one titled "Un traité manichéen retrouvé en Chine" (*Journal Asiatique* 1913) by Chavanne and Pelliot. Here I have translated the relevant passage in the *Xiuyao jing* cited in Pelliot's article, following the Japanese edition:

> "In general, the seven luminaries, in other words, the Sun, the Moon and the five stars, exert their influences over human beings. Each of them takes a turn each day, repeating in seven days. We use this [method] because the respective [seven luminaries] exert positive and negative influences over things. One should be careful when one uses this [method]. However, if one does not recall right away [the day of the week], one may ask the Central Asians, the Persians or people from the Five India-s, who should all know. The *nigaṇṭha*-s (the Jains) and the Manicheans perform ablutions on the day of *mi* 蜜 (Sunday). The Persians too make this an important day, maintaining such practices without forgetting them. Thus, the contemporary appellations of the seven luminaries of people from various countries are given as follows."

After this passage, Shi Yao gives a list explaining what the weekdays from Sunday to Saturday are in three languages. Here while "Indian name" quite certainly refers to Sanskrit, it may perhaps be hazardous to equate "Central Asian" to Sogdian, and "Persian" to Pahlavī without reservation. For the time being, let us take "Central Asian" as the Sogdian language used by the Manicheans. "Persian" is usually Pahlavī, in other words, Middle Persian. One should note that the days of the week in "Persian" are expressed by the numerals from one to seven. Such a custom is also observed in modern Arabic. At any rate, Amoghavajra must have picked these up by ear and Shi Yao wrote down how the names were pronounced by Amoghavajra as he heard them in some variety of Iranian language. To complicate the matters further, there are many variant readings when it comes to the transliteration of foreign terms by Chinese characters (see table in Fig.33).

Since the multilingual lists of the names of the weekdays in the Continental edition are found only in the second fascicle, this list was quoted by scholars from the second fascicle. However, in the Japanese version these foreign transcriptions are found even in the first fascicle at the beginning of the description of each luminary.

As shown in the above example, Sunday (day of *mi* 蜜) is considered a particularly important day among the seven planetary weekdays, each presided by their respective luminaries. In the Japanese almanac *Guchūreki* 具注暦 as well, this day was marked for easy identification. Because of that, during the late Heian period, when Sukuyōdō flourished, the character *mitsu* 蜜 was written in red in the almanacs.

Yang Jingfeng, who translated the first fascicle of the *Xiuyao jing*, probably thought that it would be troublesome to ask foreigners what day it was. Therefore, he appended a method of weekday calculation to the end of the text. As already mentioned, this is the seventh "section," the *Suanyaozhi zhang* 算曜直章, which is extant only in the Japanese edition.[44]

The *Xiuyao jing*, both first and second fascicles, describes the power of the seven luminaries under the following four groupings:

1) Actions to be undertaken on the day governed by that luminary (*zhiri* 直日); and conversely, actions not to be undertaken on that day.

2) The character and fortune of the person born on a particular weekday.

3) Major events that would take place in certain years when the fifth day of the fifth month coincides with a particular weekday.

4) The power [of the luminary] when solar or lunar eclipses, or earthquakes take place on a particular weekday.

---

[44] See Chapter Seven, p.95.

Chinese		Central Asian names (Sogdian)		Persian Names (Pahlavī numerals)		Indian names (Sanskrit)	
Sun	ri 日 taiyang 太陽	蜜	myr	耀	ēw	阿徐底耶 [1]	āditya
Moon	yue 月 taiyin 太陰	漠 [2]	m'x	婁禍 [3]	dō	蘇摩 [4]	soma
Fire	huo 火 yinghuo 熒惑	雲漠 [5]	wnx'n	勢	sě	盎誐羅迦	aṅgāraka
Water	shui 水 chenxing 辰星	咥	ṭyr	製 [6]	čahār	部陀	budha
Wood	mu 木 suixing 歲星	溫沒斯 [7]	wrmzṭ	本	panǰ	勿哩訶婆跛底	bṛhatspati
Gold	jin 金 taibai 太白	那歇 [8]	n'xyδ	數	šaš	戌羯羅 [9]	śukra
Earth	tu 土 zhenxing 鎮星	枳浣 [10]	kym'n	翕 [11]	haft	賒及以室折羅 [12]	śanaiścara

Variants: 1.T 阿儞底耶 2. K_1 寞 T 莫 3.T 婁 4. K_1 蘇摩 5. K_1 雲漢 6. K_1 & T 掣 7. K_1 鶻𠰍勿 T 鶻勿 8.K1 那頡 9.K1 戌訖羅 10. K_1 枳緩 11. K_1 欲 12. K_1 拾室悉羅

Note: T = Taishō Tripiṭaka K_1 = 1st fasc. of Kakushō ed.覚勝本. After the "Persian Name", the text continues with the word *senwu* 森勿 (= Pahlavī *šambih*).

Fig.33 Names of the seven luminaries found in the Kakushō edition of the second fascicle of the *Xiuyao jing*.

In the case of items one and two, concerning actions to be undertaken, there are many references on this subject in Sanskrit texts starting from the *Yavanajātaka,* and the material is by and large consistent with those found in the *Xiuyao jing*. By contrast, the Sanskrit source for items three and four cannot be ascertained. For item three, it may be particularly difficult to identify an Indian source, or to explain why the day of the week of the fifth day of the fifth month was given such importance.

5. Other Methods of Divination

Following the above four chapters, which focus on the two main themes of the *Xiuyao jing* (that is, the *nakṣatra*-s and the luminaries), in the fifth chapter the author tries to impart a variety of knowledge. This chapter is also where the Continental edition and the Japanese edition diverge from each other the most. In the Japanese edition, four topics are discussed in the following order:

1. Day of Amṛta (*ganlu* 甘露日) / Day of Vajraśikhara (*jingangfeng ri* 金剛峰日) / Day of Rakṣas (*luocha ri* 羅刹日)
2. Divination based on *Taibai* 太白 (Venus)
3. Six malicious *nakṣatra*-s
4. Twelve Places

In the first fascicle of the Continental edition, the second topic (Divination based on Venus) is not to be found, and the remaining topics are presented in the order three, four and one. However, in the same Continental edition, the second item, divination based on Venus, is found in the second fascicle. Incidentally, the Continental edition has a tendency to avoid overlap between the first and second fascicles, in an attempt to make the two appear as if they were one.

Among these four topics, the "Twelve Places," as mentioned earlier, is one of the basic elements of Western genethliacal astrology. However, in the *Xiuyao jing* the explanation of this topic is scant. It is not certain whether the other three originated in India or not.

Three Types of Day: Amṛta, Vajraśikhara and Rakṣas

If one tries to combine the seven luminaries with the presiding days (*zhiri* 直日) of the twenty-seven *nakṣatra*-s (correspondence between the *nakṣatra* and the day as in Fig.27), one would arrive at 189 (7×27) combinations. Among these luminary-*nakṣatra* combinations, particular ones are assigned to three categories as follows:

Amṛta	Sun	Moon	Mars	Mercury	Jupiter	Venus	Saturn
	Zhen 軫	Bi 畢	Wei 尾	Liu 柳	Gui 鬼	Fang 房	Xing 星

Vajraśikhara	Sun	Moon	Mars	Mercury	Jupiter	Venus	Saturn
	Wei 尾	Nü 女	Bi 壁	Mao 昴	Jing 井	Zhang 張	Kang 亢

Rakṣas	Sun	Moon	Mars	Mercury	Jupiter	Venus	Saturn
	Wei 尾	Gui 鬼	Yi 翼	Shen 參	Di 氐	Kui 奎	Liu 柳

Day of Amṛta: Very auspicious. Propitious for receiving consecration (*abhiṣeka*), building monastery, receiving precepts, Buddhist studies, monastic practice and taking up official positions.

Day of Vajraśikhara: Propitious for undertaking all acts of subordination, recitation of mantras of the *Ritianzi* 日天子 (*Sūryadeva*), performing *homa* rites, and making profits.

Day of Rakṣas: Unpropitious for everything. Certainly disastrous.

Judging from their content, these particular days and the methods for determining them may have originated within Esoteric Buddhism.

Divination Based on Venus (*Taibai* 太白)

The phenomenon of Venus' heliacal rising and setting, i.e., when it becomes invisible as it approaches the Sun and visible again as it moves away from the Sun, has long functioned as a basis for divination. Such examples go back as far as to the well-known "Venus tablet of *Ammisaduqa*" from Mesopotamia in the seventeenth century BCE. Divination based on the pattern of the heliacal rising and setting of Venus existed in ancient India as well. The Indians, however, did not deal exclusively with Venus like the Mesopotamians did, despite recent studies that suggest a possible relation between Indian and Mesopotamian Venusian divination.

The Venusian divination of the *Xiuyao jing* is probably unrelated to actual astronomical observation. Both fascicles of the *Xiuyao jing* describe the daily positions of Venus within a month, starting from the east, moving clockwise in eight cardinal points, and followed by the center and zenith in a ten-day cycle. The beginning and the end of the description in the text is as follows:

For each month—
1st, 11th, 21st day—East
2nd, 12th, 22nd day—Southeast
3rd, 13th, 23rd day—South
...
9th, 19th, 29th day—Centre, entering the earth
10th, 20th, 30th day—Zenith

The "ten directions" are thus conceived in a three dimensional manner. Since the direction that Venus occupies is considered auspicious, action, such as a journey, engaged in that direction is thought to be free of obstacles.

Such a method of divination has not been found in Indian texts. In China since ancient times, divination based on the five planets referred also to the heliacal rising and setting of the planets. However, they bear no relation to those found in the *Xiuyao jing*. The background and sources for the development of this method of divination remain unidentified.

Six Malefic *Nakṣatra*-s

The six malefic *nakṣatra*-s are the person's governing *nakṣatra* (Birth *Nakṣatra*) and, counting from there, the tenth, fourth, sixteenth, twentieth and thirteenth *nakṣatra*-s. Namely in respective order, these are:

Affairs (*shi* 事)
Intention (*yi* 意)
Gathering (*ju* 聚)
Unity (*tong* 同)
Adversary (*ke* 克)

If these *nakṣatra*-s are transited by the seven luminaries, disasters will arise, hence they are called the six malicious *nakṣatra*-s. Their Indian counterparts are unknown.

Twelve Places and Seven Luminaries

As mentioned earlier, the *Xiuyao jing* does not give much coverage to the Twelve Places that form the core of genethliacal astrology.

Only the auspiciousness of the seven luminaries when in the Twelve Places is given:[45]

Sun—Auspicious in the Natal Sign (*benminggong* 本命宮),[46] third, sixth and tenth places.
Moon—Auspicious in the Natal Sign, sixth, seventh and third places.
Mars—Disastrous with fire hazard in the Natal Sign.
Mercury—Auspicious in the second, fourth, eighth and tenth places.
Jupiter—Auspicious in the second, ninth and fifth places.
Venus—Auspicious in the Natal Sign, second, third, fourth, fifth, eighth and twelfth places.
Saturn—Disastrous in the Natal Sign.

Here for the first time, the term "Natal Sign" (*benminggong* 本命宮) appears, though no definition is given. From the examples in the later texts such as the *Qiyao rangzai jue*, we can see that the "Natal Sign" refers to the place of the Moon at the time of one's birth (Figs.20, 21). However, according to Morita Ryūsen (Vol.1, p.291), there appears to have been different interpretations of "Natal Sign" (*minggong* 命宮) from an early date in the history of astrology in Japan.

Incidentally, if one comes to an astrologer not knowing what his "Natal *Nakṣatra*" (not "Natal Sign") was, what could then be done? This is the question posed at the end of the chapter. Here, Yang Jingfeng remarks that a person who does not know his or her own birthday would not know the correct "Birth *Nakṣatra.*" In this case, the following method may be used. First, when the client comes to see the astrologer, the astrologer observes which part of the body the person's hand touches. Each body part from head to feet corresponds to one of the twenty-eight *nakṣatra*-s (not found in the second fascicle). A similar correspondence is also found in the *Qiyao rangzai jue*, in which the *nakṣatra*-s are visualized in connection with the human body (Fig.34 from Morita). The *nakṣatra*-body correspondence in the *Xiuyao jing* is almost identical to that in the *Qiyao rangzai jue*, with the exceptions that left and right are largely reversed and that *Ārdrā* (*Shen* 參), *Punarvasū* (*Jing* 井), and *Puṣya* (*Gui* 鬼) correspond to the eyes, ears and teeth respectively.

[45] This topic is called *gocara* in Sanskrit texts. Cf. *Bṛhatsaṃhitā* 103.

[46] Author's note: I want to correct my interpretation of the "The Natal Sign" in my Japanese book. Instead of the Ascendent, it should refer to the place of the Moon at birth.

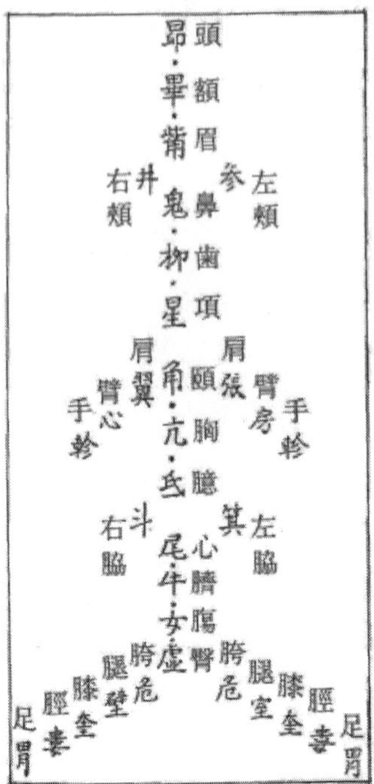

Fig.34 The 28 *Nakṣatra*-s and the body parts (from *Qiyao rangzai jue*).

This way of correlating the stars and the human body originated in Western astrology. In Western astrology, the twelve zodiacal signs from Aries to Pisces when connected to the human body from head to feet form what is known as the Zodiacal Man (Fig.35).[47] While there are various representations, let us examine the one proposed by Manilius (first half of the first century CE):[48]

[47] Note that the Chinese version of the Zodiacal man, corresponding to the western one in which the head is represented by Aries, takes *Kṛttikā* as the head which reflects the old Indian *nakṣatra*-system.

[48] *Astronomica* 2.453–465.

Head	Aries
Neck	Taurus
Arms	Gemini
Breast	Cancer
Sides and shoulders	Leo
Thighs	Sagittarius
Knees	Capricorn
Shanks	Aquarius
Belly	Virgo
Loins	Libra
Groin	Scorpio
Thighs	Sagittarius
Knees	Capricorn
Shanks	Aquarius
Feet	Pisces

This idea was quickly transmitted to India through the *Yavanajātaka*. In Varāhamihira's *Bṛhajjātaka*, the following example is given:

Head	Aries
Mouth	Taurus
Throat	Gemini
Arms	Cancer
Heart	Leo
Abdomen	Virgo
Lower abdomen	Libra
Genitalia	Scorpio
Upper legs	Sagittarius
Knees	Capricorn
Shanks	Aquarius
Feet	Pisces

This kind of Zodiacal Man had its origin in Egypt, where medical science and astrology were connected to each other. A work titled *Iatromathematica* (medical astrology) is found in the *Liber Hermetis*, a text said to originate in Egypt. The basic idea behind medical astrology is that the universe, the macrocosm, is analogous to the microcosm that the human being represents. The universe was believed to be a living being that constantly influences human beings. As the twelve zodiacal signs, i.e., the zodiac belt, came to play an important role in astrology, the zodiac itself became considered as an organic living being.

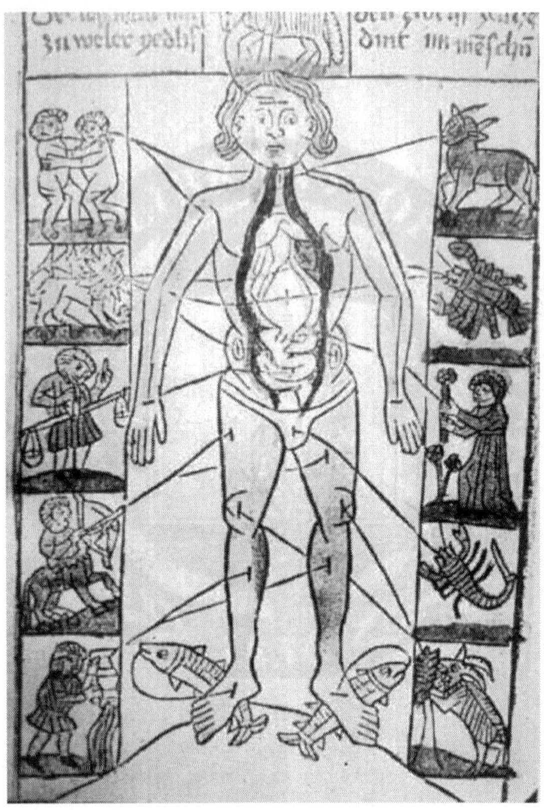

Fig.35 Zodiacal Man from the Calendar of Regiomontanus, ca.1475.
(http://www.nlm.nih.gov/exhibition/harrypottersworld/images/details/OB0056.jpg)

A similar relationship between the cosmic man and the earthly man was a mythological theme in ancient India. In the "Hymn of Puruṣa" (*Puruṣasūkta*) of the *Ṛgveda*, the gigantic *puruṣa* (the Primordial Man) was separated into parts while the creation of the universe was described. At the micro level, the word *puruṣa* means "human being."

Against such a background, the Zodical Man and the medical astrology of the West were easily Indianized. In Indian astrological works, this is called *kāla-puruṣa* (*kāla* means "time"), with the twelve zodiacal signs corresponding to the body parts. Utpala (tenth century), in his commentary to *Bṛhajjātaka* 1.4, writes:

> "If, at the time of birth, the zodiacal sign (*rāśi*) corresponding to the bodily part of the *puruṣa* called *kāla*, was transited by an inauspicious star (*pāpagrahâkrāntaḥ*), the child given birth to will have a defect in that body part—thus [the astrologer] should say."[49]

What is special about the *kāla-puruṣa* in the *Xiuyao jing* is that it connects the body with the twenty-eight *nakṣatra*-s instead of the twelve zodiacal signs, with *Kṛttikā* (*Mao* 昴) being the head. As we have seen before in the Indian text, Aries (*Meṣa*) corresponds to the head and the beginning of Aries usually corresponds to *Aśvinī* (*Lou* 婁) as shown in Fig.25 (p.52). In the *Xiuyao jing*, although the beginning of "Aries" corresponds to *Aśvinī* (*Lou*), the *nakṣatra*-s always start from *Kṛttikā* (*Mao*) whenever the *nakṣatra*-s are described, whether in the twenty-seven or twenty-eight *nakṣatra* system. In other words, in the older tradition, *Kṛttikā* (*Mao*) was always taken as the start of the *nakṣatra*-s. However, in the newer astrology that had originated in the West, *Aśvinī* (*Lou*) was taken as the start instead. The *kāla-puruṣa* in the *Xiuyao jing* is thus a hybrid of the old and the new.

---

[49] *janmakāle yo rāśiḥ pāpagrahākrāntaḥ sa kālākhyasya puruṣasya yasminn aṅge sthitas tatrāṅge jātasyopaghāto vaktavyaḥ* ||

6. The Auspiciousness of Individual Days

The last topic of the first fascicle of the *Xiuyao jing* of Amoghavajra deals with the auspiciousness of individual days. Since that topic is discussed also at the beginning of the second fascicle, and since the section known as "*Suanyaozhi zhang*" 算曜直章 is missing at the end of the first fascicle in the Continental edition, the reader may have the impression that the first fascicle continues on to the second fascicle. This is one of the reasons why the two fascicles have been mistaken as one text.

If one examines closely the relevant passages in the two fascicles, one can see that the material is identical and even the verses quoted in both are the same. In the Continental edition, Chapter Six of the first fascicle stops in the middle, and the remaining half was made into "Chapter Seven—Explanation Concerning Auspiciousness and Inauspiciousness" 序日名善惡品第七. This division is not found in the Japanese edition.

Tithi as Time Unit

In India, a (synodic) month is divided into two halves:

> Bright half (Skt. *śuklapakṣa*, *baifen* 白分)—from the first to the fifteenth *tithi*.
>
> Dark half (Skt. *kṛṣṇapakṣa*, *heifen* 黑分)—from the sixteenth to the thirtieth *tithi*.

"Bright half" (Skt. *śukla-pakṣa*) is the half-month from the first day of the month in a lunar calendar, or astronomically the day after the conjunction of the Sun and the Moon, until the full moon; "Dark half" (Skt. *kṛṣṇa-pakṣa*) is the half-month from the day after the full moon to conjunction. Since one synodic month (Ch. *shuowangyue* 朔望月) is approximately 29.5 days, a month in a luni-solar calendar consists of either twenty-nine or thirty days.

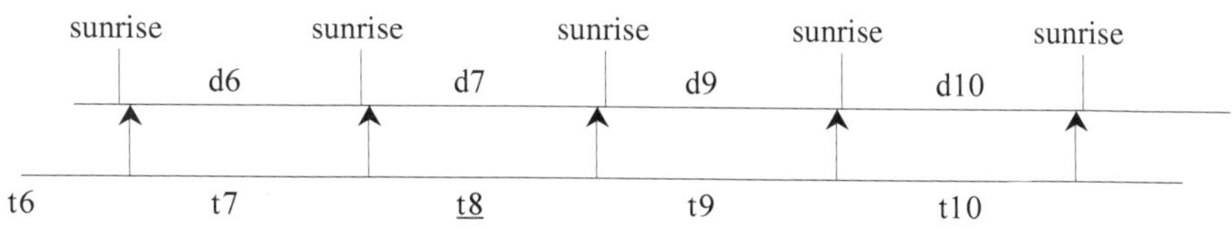

Fig.36 "Omitted day".

In the Indian calendar system, a unit called *tithi* was introduced as a measurement in relation to the length of a month. A *tithi* is defined as one thirtieth of a synodic month, or one fifteenth of a half-month. Since a true synodic month is usually just short of thirty days, a *tithi* is slightly shorter than a day (rarely the opposite happens and this was taken into consideration in a later period). Unlike the civil day, which starts from sunrise, the *tithi* divisions start from the conjunction. As a result, the point when one *tithi* changes to the next shifts slightly every day.

For instance, as in Fig.36, if the sixth *tithi* (t6) is current at sunrise, the day is called the "sixth day" (d6). In this example, the day (d7) contains the ending points of the two *tithi*-s (t7 and t8) and at sunrise of the following day (d9), the ninth *tithi* (t9) is current. Thus the eighth *tithi* in this example is not named for a civil day and the eighth day (d8) is thus omitted. This omitted day is called the *kṣayadina* or *avama* in Sanskrit. The calculation of the "omitted day," along with the intercalary months, is extremely important in Indian calendrics.

Besides determining the number of days in a month (i.e., twenty-nine or thirty), the *tithi* also plays an important role in the everyday life. This is because religious ceremonies are performed according to the *tithi*-s, which determine the auspiciousness of a day. To be precise, the auspicious and inauspicious "days" in the *Xiuyao jing* should be *tithi*-s instead. However, as it is explained:

> Bright half (*baifen* 白分)—from the first to the fifteenth day.
> Dark half (*heifen* 黑分)—from the sixteenth to the thirtieth day.

In the *Xiuyao jing*, "days" and *tithi*-s are not distinguished from each other.

The auspiciousness of the bright and dark halves, each containing fifteen "days," is versified as follows (based on the Kakushō edition):

一三五七十　十一與十三
於二白黑分　所作皆成就
黑三夜七晝　十夜十四晝
白四夜八晝　一夜十五晝
於此白黑分　晝夜不成就
日中及中夜　已後皆通吉

First, third, fifth, seventh, tenth, eleventh and thirteenth,
in the two halves bright and dark, all that is done would be propitious,
dark third night and seventh day, tenth night and fourteenth day,
bright fourth night and eighth day, first <emend. eleventh> night and fifteenth day.
In these days and nights of the dark and the bright halves, things are unpropitious.
After midday and midnight, everything is auspicious.

This verse is expressed pithily for the purpose of mnemonic, albeit at the expense of comprehensibility; a prose explanation is additionally given in both the first and second fascicles. According to that, in both the bright and dark half-month, activities performed on the first, third, fifth, seventh, tenth, eleventh and thirteen day will yield success, while those performed on the third night, seventh day, tenth night, fourteenth day of the dark half and the fourth night, eighth day, eleventh (the text reads "first") night and the fifteenth day will not. The days described here are from sunrise to midday, and the nights are from sunset to midnight. After midday and midnight everything is auspicious, as explained in the last line (Fig.37). The unmarked days are the ordinary days whose auspiciousness is determined by the *nakṣatra*-s and the luminaries of the respective days.

Day		1	2	3	4	5	6	7	8	9	10	11	12	13	14	15
Bright half	Day	O		O		O		O	×		O	O		O		×
	Night	O		O	×	O		O			O	×		O		
Dark half	Day	O		O		O		×			O	O		O	×	
	Night	O		×		O		O			×	O		O		

Fig.37 Success (O) and Failure (×).

The auspiciousness of *tithi* as described in the Indian texts and in the *Xiuyao jing* is more or less the same. However, as mentioned before, since the Indian *tithi* is different from the ordinary day and the daily transition points of *tithi* are not fixed, it is not correct to express half-*tithi* as a half-day. In India, a half-*tithi* is known as a *karaṇa*, an important concept in astrology. The system described here in the *Xiuyao jing* is thus an unsuccessful attempt to translate this unique feature of the Indian system.

Names and Presiding Deities of *Tithi*-s

In the *Xiuyao jing*, moreover, three items—namely, 1) name, 2) presiding deity, and 3) things to be done—are given for each day from the first to the fifteenth day, with no distinction between the bright and the dark halves. This is very similar to Garga's system, as quoted in Utpala's commentary to Ch.98 of the *Bṛhatsaṃhitā*—"Tithikarmaguṇa" (Characteristics of Activities in [Each] *Tithi*):

	Name in *Xiuyao jing*		Name in Garga's passage	
1	建日	starting day	Pratipad	beginning
2	德財	virtuous wealth	Bhadrā	auspicious
3	威力	might	Balā	strong
4	惡業	bad karma	Riktā	futile
5	圓滿	perfection	Pūrṇā	full
6	求名	fame-seeking	Māsā	lunar (?)
7	朋友	friends	Mitrā	friendly
8	力戰	fierce battle	Mahābalā	powerful
9	兇猛	ferociously hostile	Ugrasenā	with a strong army
10	善法*	good dharma	Sudhanvā	having an excellent bow
11	慈猛	extremely friendly	Sunandā	pleasing
12	名聞	famed	Yamā	Yama's
13	最勝	utmost victorious	Jayā	victorious
14	勇猛	ferociously brave	Ugrā	terrible
15	吉相	auspicious	Siddhārthā	wish-fulfilling

(Note: All the names are in feminine form because they modify *tithi* which is a feminine noun. *10 could be interpreted as *sudharmā*, which was translated as "good dharma" (善法 *shanfa*).)

While there are some doubts concerning items 6 and 12 above, the Chinese and the Sanskrit for the rest correspond completely to each other.

Presiding Deities

In the *Xiuyao jing*, each *tithi* is assigned a presiding deity. However, the treatment of their names is different in the two fascicles. In the second fascicle, Sanskrit names are given in Chinese transcriptions while their Chinese names are given as interlinear notes with the remark, "known in the Tang [Period] as..." (唐云 *tangyun*). In the first fascicle, the Chinese names are given with the "Sanskrit pronunciation" provided as interlinear notes. This is another difference between the first translation and the retranslation. The content corresponds closely to Garga's system mentioned earlier. Discrepancies between Chinese and Sanskrit in the table below are indicated by *.

	Xiuyao jing first fascicle	*Xiuyao jing* second fascicle	Garga
1	梵王 Brahma	鉢 諸 鉢 底 *Prajāpati (Lord of creation)	*Svayambhū
2	造化神	苾利訶娑鉢底 Bṛhaspati	Bṛhaspati
3	那羅延 Nārāyaṇa	毘紐 Viṣṇu	Viṣṇu
4	閻羅王	閻謨 Yama	Yama
5	月天子	蘇謨 Soma (Moon)	Soma
6	童子天 Kumāra	摩羅 Kumāra	Kumāra
7	北斗 North Dipper	七仙 Saptarṣayaḥ (Seven sages)	Saptarṣayaḥ
8	婆藪神	婆娑 Vasava	Vasavaḥ
9	毗舍闍鬼 Piśāca	嚕達囉尼 Rudrāṇī	Rudrāṇī
10	善法神 Sudharma	達謨 Sudharma	Dharma
11	自在天 Iśvara	嚕捺嚧 Rudra	Kāmaśatru
12	日天子	阿逸都 Āditya (Sun)	Āditya
13	天魔王	鉢折底 *Piśāca	*Kāma
14	藥叉將	藥葝 *Yakṣa	*Rudra
15	魂靈神	多盧 Pitaraḥ (Ancestors)	Pitaraḥ

Presiding deities of *tithi*/day.

The various propitious activities for different days described in the Indian texts are not much different from those described in the *Xiuyao jing*.[50]

[50] As I have no intention to confuse the readers with the bewildering details, I shall limit my explanation to the above. Those who are interested in the details should refer to Taishō(1299)21.393–94.

7. Calculation of the Weekdays

The entire *Xiuyao jing* attributed to Amoghavajra has been described above. The astrology of the text is based on the traditional twenty-seven *nakṣatra* system of India, together with the astrology based on the seven luminaries that originated in the West. In India, this astrology was becoming popular but was still relatively new. These constitute the two main topics of the *Xiuyao jing*. As such, the title *Xiuyao jing* accurately reflects its contents (*nakṣatra*-s and luminaries).

The twenty-seven *nakṣatra*-s in the text were readily accepted due to their similarity to the twenty-eight Chinese lodges. On the other hand, the concept of seven luminaries was first transmitted to China at around the same time as when the *Xiuyao jing* was being composed, and furthermore this was a new concept in divination and calendar-making. Yang Jingfeng, who retranslated the *Xiuyao jing*, knew that a method of calculation of weekdays based on the luminaries could be found in an Indian astronomical text known as the *Jiuzhi li* 九執曆. Thus he must have thought that this method of calculation should be added to the end of the *Xiuyao jing*. Amoghavajra too might have agreed to this. This appended text is known as "Section Seven"—the "Xiuyao jing suanyaozhi zhang diqi" 宿曜經算曜直章第七 as mentioned earlier.

Section Seven and the *Jiuzhi li*

This chapter is missing in the Continental editions and is found only in the Japanese manuscipts. As the material is extremely interesting from a historical point of view, the somewhat lengthy text is quoted here in its entirety, based on the Kakushō edition and the Tōji manuscript. The punctuations are the author's.

宿曜經算曜直章第七 <此非文殊所說。故不言品、別起云章也。>天竺曆瞿曇氏所譯本云、是大梵天所造。五通仙人傳授推求。今於歷經、略此一章、附於宿曜之後。置曆上元癸丑、至今大唐開元二年甲寅歳、積一千五百一算外。<若推已[51]後每年加一算。若推已前每年減一算。>以十二乘入元岠求年積算。又加自入年已來月數。<起二月加之、假令推五月五日、更加三[52]算、是也。> 加訖、重張。下位以七乘之、以二百二十八除之、為積閏。不盡為閏餘。以積閏加上位。加訖、置為積月。以三十乘積月。 又加入月已來日數。加訖、重張之。以十一乘下位、加差五百、以七百三除之。所得為小月日。不盡為小餘。以小月日減上位。減訖、置為積日位。以六十去積日。不盡者、令起甲辰、算上則所求年月日之甲子乙丑他。又以七去積日、不盡者、令起太陰、以次火水木金土日。算盡之上則是其日所得曜直也。

右惣六品一章修成一卷

Section Seven, *Xiuyao jing*, “Calculation of the Weekday.” <This is not proclaimed by Mañjuśī and is therefore not called “chapter” (*pin*) but “section” (*zhang*) instead.> According to the Indian calendar translated by Gautama, [its content] was composed by the Great Brahmā, and the *Wutong xianren* (lit. sages of the full understanding of five[53]) transmitted the text and made use of the calculation. A section was abridged from the astronomical text and appended to the end of the *Xiuyao* [*jing*]. One sets the astronomical epoch to the year Guichou. From this year to the second year of Kaiyuan i.e. Jiayin, of the Great Tang, 1501 years have expired. <For calculation after that, add one for each year; for calculation before that, subtract one for each year.> Multiply the number of years from the epoch by twelve and add the number of months from the beginning of the present year. <The addition counts from the second month. Assuming it is the fifth day of the fifth month, one then adds three.> After the addition, place the value in two positions.[54] Multiply the value “below” by 7 and divide it by 228 to obtain the sum of intercalary months (*adhimāsagaṇa*). The remainder is the *runyu* (*adhimāsaśeṣa*). Add the sum of

---

[51] Emended by Yano. In the Kakushō ed., all *yi* 已 read as *ji* 巳. In *Kaiyuan zhan jing*, *xiang* 向.

[52] Originally 四, emended to 三 by Yano.

[53] Translator’s note: As *Jiuzhi li* shares a number of features with the *Pañcasiddhāntika* (lit. “Five Astronomical Treatises”), both Yabuuti and Pingree were in the opinion that the “five” refers to the Indian text. On the other hand, Niu had argued that the term refers generically to the Indian *ṛṣi*-s as they were believed to have mastered the five supernatural powers as well as the Vedic lore including astronomy (Niu Weixing 钮卫星 . 2007. “Wutongxianren kao” 五通仙人 *Shanghai Jiaotongdaxue xuebao* (*zhexue shehui kexue ban*) 上海交通大学学报(哲学社会科学版) 5:37–44.

intercalary months to the value "above." After the addition, it becomes the sum of months from the Epoch (*māsagaṇa*). Multiply the sum of months from the epoch by 30. Add the number of days from the beginning of the present month. After the addition, place the value in two positions. Multiply the value "below" by 11, add 500 and divide it by 703. The result is the *xiaoyueri* 小月日 (*avama*). The reminder is the *xiaoyu* 小餘 (*avamaśeṣa*). Subtract *xiaoyueri* from the value "above." After the subtraction, place it where the sum of days from the Epoch (*ahargaṇa*) is. Divide the sum of days from the Epoch by 60. If it does not divide out completely, then one counts starting from *Jiachen* 甲辰, and one obtains through the calculation the sexagenary day such as, *Jiazi* 甲子, *Yichou* 乙丑 and so on. Divide the sum of days from the Epoch by 7. The remainder [corresponds to the weekday], beginning with the Moon, followed by Mars, Mercury, Jupiter, Venus, Saturn and Sun. Counting the remainders, the weekday would be [the day in question].

The above six chapters and one section are compiled into one fascicle

Firstly, this part of the text is called a "*zhang*" 章 instead of a "*pin*" 品 unlike the preceding six chapters: the readers are reminded by the interlinear note that this is because the text was not proclaimed by the Bodhisattva Mañjuśrī. As far as the source of the text is concerned, it is said to be the Indian calendar (*Tianzhu li* 天竺曆) translated by Gautama 瞿曇氏. As mentioned earlier (p.55), this is none other than the *Jiuzhi li* 九執曆 (718 CE) of Gautamasiddha 瞿曇悉達. In fact, the content of this "section" is entirely based on the *Jiuzhi li* and even the expressions are largely borrowed from it. In the passage above, the expressions identical to those in the *Jiuzhi li* are underlined.

The *Jiuzhi li* corresponds to fascicle 104 of a much larger textual compilation of 120 fascicles known as the *Kaiyuan zhanjing* 開元占經. As a collection of old Chinese astral materials, the *Kaiyuan zhanjing* is an extremely important work. The text was lost soon after the Tang period and was rediscovered toward the end of Ming period inside a Buddhist statue. It was incorporated in the *Siku quanshu* 四庫全書 compiled during the Qing period. Thanks to the research of Professor Yabuuti Kiyosi in

---

[54] Translator's note: *Chongzhang* 重張 refers the practice of copying a value into two places, upper and lower, expressed usually in Sanskrit as *pṛthak*. The value in the lower place is used for further calculation, while the value in the upper placed will be saved for later operation. As such the punctuation in the Chinese text is emended accordingly.

the mid-twentieth century, the mathematical astronomy of the *Jiuzhi li* is now properly understood. When I had the opportunity to study Indian astronomy under Professor Yabuuti, the *Jiuzhi li* was among the taught subjects. About ten years later, I had the chance again to assist the professor to revise his English translation of the *Jiuzhi li*.[55] The text has therefore left an indelible impression on me.

When the author discovered that this text survived in the Japanese edition of *Xiuyao jing*, albeit in fragments, needless to say it was a big surprise. Anyone with a basic knowledge of Indian astronomy can understand the calculation method described there. It was, however, not properly understood by Morita, who said in his monumental *Mikkyō senseihō* (Vol.1, p.126). "This [chapter] was probably written by [Yang] Jingfeng himself, using advanced mathematics and is extremely difficult to comprehend."

Calculation of Weekdays

To determine the day of the week, one first calculates the total number of the days from the Epoch (Ch. *liyuan*, Jp. *rekigen* 暦元, the reference starting day for calendrical calculation). Then this number is divided by seven to obtain the remainder. If the remainder is one, the weekday would be the same as that of the Epoch.[56] The remainders two through six correspond to the following weekdays respectively. If the number of days since the epoch is divisible by seven, the day in question is then the weekday before that of the epoch. In the same way, by obtaining the remainder from dividing the sum of days since the epoch by sixty, one can determine the sexagenary stem-branch (Ch. *ganzhi*, Jp. *edo* 干支) of the day.

Let us now look at how the sum of the days since the epoch is calculated in Indian astronomical texts.[57] It is customary to first set the Epoch on the first day of the *śukla-pakṣa* of the month *Caitra* (translated as *jueyue* 角月 in the *Xiuyao jing*), which coincides with the vernal equinox in the distant past. From the Epoch down to the year when the day is calculated, a total number of Y years have passed. Within the current year, m months have passed. Within the current month up to and

[55] Yabuuti, Kiyosi. 1979. "Researches on the *Chiu-chih li:* Indian Astronomy under the T'ang Dynasty." *Acta Asiatica* 36.

[56] On the weekday of the Epoch, see below.

[57] Yabuuti 1979:13–15.

including the present day, t days (*tithi*, to be precise) have passed. Note that Y and m are counted "exclusively," while t is counted "inclusively."

First, calculate (A), the sum of intercalary months from the epoch, with the following formula.

$$A = \frac{(Y \times 12 + m) \times 7 + k_1}{228} \quad \ldots\ldots (1)$$

This formula assumes that one solar year has twelve months and that seven intercalary months are needed for every 228 solar months, or every nineteen years. In other words, nineteen solar years are roughly equivalent to 235 synodic months. This is the well-known "Metonic Cycle," the intercalary cycle of the luni-solar calendar.[58]

Since the intercalary cycle does not necessarily start on the Epoch, one must add a fraction of the cycle as the Epoch constant. This is k_1 in formula (1). To calculate this constant, obtain the sum of intercalary months (A) and take only the integer portion of the result. The remainder is called "*runyu*" 閏餘 (Skt. *adhimāsaśeṣa*). Then, calculate the sum of synodic months from the Epoch (M) with the following formula:

$$M = (Y \times 12 + m) + [A] \quad \ldots\ldots(2)$$

[ ] means only the integer portion is taken.

With the value obtained above, calculate the sum of "omitted days" (*ūnarātra*, *avama* or *kṣayadina*, see p.91) (U) with the following formula:

$$U = \frac{(M \times 30 + t) \times 11 + k_2}{703} \quad \ldots\ldots (3)$$

What this formula means is that, assuming one synodic month has exactly 30 "days," a number of "omitted days" (Ch. *qianri*, Jp. *ketsujitsu* 欠日) at the ratio of 11 days per 703 "days" are needed, alternatively expressed in the number of "short months" of 29 days (here the "day" is in fact *tithi*). k_2 is the Epoch constant as in formula (1). In this case as well, take only the integer part of the result. The remainder is called the "small remainder" or *xiaoyu* 小餘 (Skt. *avamaśeṣa*). Now, finally, calculate the sum of the days (D) from the Epoch with the following formula:

---

[58] See p.26.

$$D = (M \times 30 + t) - [U] \;\ldots\ldots\; (4)$$

If one understands the explanation so far, with the knowledge of elementary mathematics, even those who are not conversant in classical Chinese should be able to interpret the "Suanyaozhi zhang" as quoted above. No one would consider this advanced mathematics.

The Epoch constants used in the "Suanyaozhi zhang" are:

$k_1 = 0 \qquad k_2 = 500$

To sum, the procedure described in the text is as follows:

$$A = \frac{(Y \times 12 + m) \times 7}{228} \;\ldots\ldots\; (1)$$

$$M = (Y \times 12 + m) + [A] \;\ldots\ldots\; (2)$$

$$U = \frac{(M \times 30 + t) \times 11 + 500}{703} \;\ldots\ldots\; (3)$$

$$D = (M \times 30 + t) - [U] \;\ldots\ldots\; (4)$$

Epoch

Let us now examine the problem of the Epoch. Yang Jingfeng calculated the sum of the years from the Epoch to the second year of *Kaiyuan* (sexagesimally *jiayin* 甲寅, 714 CE), to be 1501 years. In other words, the Epoch was 788 BCE. In Yang's words, the sexagesimal placement of this year was *guichou* 癸丑. Moreover, his model follows the Indian calendar by making the day of the Epoch the new Moon day of the second month (*eryue shuori* 二月朔日). Let us try to determine what month and day this would be in the Julian calendar. According to the text, the answer is determined by first subtracting the integer multiples of sixty from the sum of the days: a remainder of one, two, three corresponds to *jiachen* 甲辰, *yisi* 乙巳, or *bingwu* 丙午 and so on. If the remainder is one, the sexagenary day at the Epoch would be "*jiachen*." In a similar way, the remainder from the integer multiples of seven corresponds to Monday and so on. The weekday of the Epoch is therefore a Monday. Following that, one may want to find out whether "*jiachen*" and Monday coincide at around the time of vernal equinox in 788 BCE. It turns out that the day is exactly March 26th of the Julian Calendar (Julian day number 1433691). According to a computerized table of Moon phases, the new Moon was at 7:33 p.m., 25th March, 788 BCE in Babylonia;[59] in China, this was just past midnight on the 26th. Therefore, it is certain that Yang Jingfeng was the one who made this date the Epoch. However, since there is still room for greater accuracy for the Epoch constants and the two coefficients (7/228 and 11/703), if one places the Epoch at such a point in the distant past, discrepancies naturally arise. Precisely because of this, in Varāhamihira's *Pañcasiddhāntikā*, one of the Indian astronomical works that made use of such values, Śaka 428 (505 CE), a year closer to the author's time was adopted instead of the remote past. In fact, subsequent Indian astronomers have also tried to improve on these figures.

It is therefore not a problem that in the *Jiuzhi li* the new moon day of the *śuklapakṣa* of the second month of the second year of *Xianqing* 顯慶 (657 CE) was made the Epoch, fifty-seven years before the work was composed. However, even though the *Jiuzhi li* was available to Yang Jingfeng, who had in fact copied it, Yang pushed the Epoch to a date in the distant past instead. Apparently, Yang Jingfeng had only a superficial knowledge of the matter and he certainly had not thought of the great trouble he would bring to Japanese monks a thousand years later.

The fact that the "Suanyaozhi zhang" is missing in the Continental edition despite the fact that Yang Jingfeng had certainly appended it to the end of the *Xiuyao jing* may suggests that it was deliberately deleted by Chinese scholars who noticed that the calculation was not working properly. In retrospect, as a result of the deletion of this section, Yang Jingfeng's edition could not be criticized by its readers and therefore lived on in China.

When the *Xiuyao jing* was brought from China to Japan by Kūkai, only forty years had passed from the time it was completed. Naturally, the version he transmitted predates the deletion of the "Suanyaozhi zhang." It is therefore only logical that the Tōji manuscript, one of the oldest manuscripts, contains this section, as one simply does not delete something haphazardly from a precious text brought from China. While the "Suanyaozhi zhang" continued to baffle monks, it was passed down until the present day and was even described as "advanced mathematics" by a scholarly monk in the twentieth century.

---

[59] Goldstine 1973.

What about Kūkai himself, then? While one cannot say with absolute certainty whether Kūkai understood the text, some evidence for speculation is provided by a folio inserted at the end of the second fascicle of the Kakushō edition of the *Xiuyao jing*. There, the first Sundays (Ch. *miri,* Jp. *mitsujitsu* 蜜日) of the first month of the three years starting from the first year of *Yuanhe* 元和 (806–07 CE) of the Tang period are noted. The first year of *Yuanhe* is the twenty-fifth year of *Enryaku* 延暦 (which began in 806 CE) in Japan. In the fifth month of that year, the era name was changed to *Daidō* 大同. It was during the autumn of this first year of *Daidō* (806 CE) that Kūkai returned to Japan.

To sum up this record:

> Second day of the first month <*dingmao* 丁卯> of the twenty-fifth year of *Enryaku* <*bingxu* 丙戌> (806 CE)
>
> Third day of the first month <*renchen* 壬辰> of the second year of *Daidō* <*dinghai* 丁亥> (807 CE)
>
> Seventh day of the first month (Kakushō ed.: second month) <*jichou* 己丑> of the third year of *Daidō* <*xuzi* 戌子> (808 CE)

For the entry for the third year of *Daidō*, "second month" was written. As noted in the header of the manuscript, since the seventh day of the second month is a Tuesday, it should be emended as the "first month" instead. With the amendment, one would get the dates for the first Sundays of the first month of the three years, which further supports this emendation. Moreover, as mentioned in the text, since the twelfth month of the first year of *Daidō* was a "big month" in Japan whereas it was a "small month" in China, the first Sunday of the first month of the following year in China was in fact the fourth day.[60]

Who then was the one who wrote down these dates in the additional folio? According to Kakushō, the records were found in both an old text from the Muryōjuin 無量壽院 collection in Kōyasan, as well as in a manuscript belonging to Hakkōin 發光院:

> "In my opinion, our Great Master [Kūkai] at that time wrote down the weekdays (*chokuyō* 直曜) for three years as an introduction to the Section on Weekday Computation (*Suanyao zhang* 算曜章) for the benefit of those who do not understand it. For that reason, I [Kakushō] supplied it here."

---

[60] For historical calendars in Japan, see 内田正男:『日本暦日原典』; in China, 董作賓:『中國年曆簡譜』.

For the reasons mentioned above, it would be closer to the truth to say instead of "for the benefit of those who do not understand it" as Kakushō said, that this was "because one does not get the correct result based on the *Suanyaozhi zhang*." Otherwise, I agree with Kakushō on the remaining points. While Kukai was in China, he probably learned when the first Sunday of the first month of the twenty-fifth year of *Enryaku* was. If a calendar was available to him or if he knew about the methods behind calendar making, he would have easily known when the first Sundays of the following year or the year after that were. In other words, the records of the first Sundays of these three years are not the results calculated from the *Suanyaozhi zhang*; they are instead Kūkai's "souvenirs" from China.

In this way, the concept of the weekdays was brought to Japan. The question of when this concept was first used has been discussed by many scholars. In an essay by Ishida, a list of annotated almanacs (*guchūreki*) with planetary weekdays is provided.[61] The oldest among these almanacs is the one used for the diary of Fujiwara no Michinaga 藤原道長, which starts from the fourth year of *Chōtoku* 長徳 (998 CE).[62] One may recall that it was in 806 CE when the *Xiuyao jing*, whose main topic among other things was the seven luminaries, was brought to Japan. Planetary weekdays must have taken some years to become popular and to be incorporated as annotations to the almanacs.

Chapter Three—Additional Notes

(1) On the Twenty-Eight and Twenty-Seven Lunar Mansions

After the *Xiuyao jing* was brought into Japan, the twenty-seven lunar mansions were adopted. It is unknown to me whether the twenty-eight lunar mansions were adopted in the annotated calendars prior to that. Among the annotated calendars where the lunar mansions are indicated, the best known one was that of the *Mido Kanpakuki* of Fujiwara no Michinaga.[63] As an example which I gave in my book (Yano 2004), from the eight days starting from the twenty-second day of the first month of the second year of *Chōhō* 長保 (Thursday, 29 February,

---

[61] Ishida 1967. "The Annotated Almanacs (*guchūreki*) marked with the character *mitsu* 蜜 on Sundays." 日曜に『蜜』字を標記した具注暦.

[62] An older record of annotated almanac is noted in the work of Fujiwara Tadahira 藤原忠平, the great-grandfather Fujiwara no Tadahira as noted in Yano 2004.

[63] Yano 2004:139.

1000 CE), the mansions were enumerated from *Wei* 尾 to *Bi* 壁, while *Niu* 牛 was missing. When I had the opportunity to examine the original copies of the *Mido Kanpakuki*, I could verify, beside the above example, how the lunar mansions and weekdays were assigned to all the dates and found that in all cases *Niu* was missing. Moreover, the lunar mansions for the days were in fact identical to those of the "Yuexiu bangtong li" 月宿傍通曆 (Fig.27). In other words, the lunar mansions used by Michinaga in the annotated calendar belongs to the twenty-seven *nakṣatra* system of the *Xiuyao jing*.

On the other hand, since the twenty-eight lunar mansions were commonplace in China, the original *Xiuyao jing* that had used the twenty-seven lunar mansions was gradually converted into a version that used the twenty-eight-lodge system. Such is a typical example of the sinicization of Indian astrology.

In Japan, even after the astrological school *Sukuyōdō* went out of fashion, up until when the *Senmyōreki* calendar was abolished, the twenty-seven-mansion system was used. An example of the conversion of the twenty-seven mansions (*nakṣatra*-s) into the Chinese twenty-eight mansions (lodges) may be seen in the work of Shibukawa Shunkai 渋川春海, creator of the *Jōkyōreki* 貞享暦 (protagonist of the recent, acclaimed movie *Tenchimeisatsu* 天地明察). Shibukawa assigned the lunar lodge *Xing* 星 to the first day of the first month of the second year of *Jōkyō* (4 February 1685 CE).[64]

While it is common to find twenty-eight lunar mansions in the Japanese almanacs of recent years, those that use twenty-seven mansions or a mixture of twenty-eight and twenty-seven-mansions may also be found. For example, in the almanac of Dazaifu Tenmangū 太宰府天満宮 of Kyūshū both are included: the twenty-eight mansions are indicated as "new," while the twenty-seven mansions are indicated as "old." In this calendar, following the twenty-eight-mansion system, the lunar mansion *Wei* 尾 was assigned to 1 January 2013 (Tuesday). After the *Jōkyōreki* calendar, the assignment of lunar mansions was naturally continuous. Since twenty-eight is a multiple of seven, the relationship between the lunar mansions and the weekdays remains unchanged. In the example mentioned above, after twenty-eight days on 29 January 2013, it will be, once again, the lunar mansion *Wei* and a Tuesday.

---

[64] Item 10 of Fig.23.

On the other hand, whenever the twenty-seven mansions were used, it is clear that the "Yuexiu bangtong li" of the *Xiuyao jing* was followed. This can be ascertained by, for example, examining the fifteenth day of the second month of the lunar calendar: regardless of year, the mansion *Jiao* 角 is always assigned.

(2) Six Malefic *Nakṣatra*-s

While the Indian equivalents corresponding to the Six Malicious *Nakṣatra*-s are unknown to me, the wrong Chinese characters in the old edition have now been corrected. In the Kakushō edition, variant characters are given. I checked the old manuscripts and I believe that the text is correct now.

(3) Twelve Places and Seven Luminaries

When compared to those mentioned in the *Qiyao rangzai jue*, the auspiciousness and inauspiciousness of the seven luminaries in the Twelve Places mentioned in this book turn out to be different in a few occasions.[65]

(4) On the Presiding Deities of the *Tithi*-s

The Chinese translations of the presiding deities of the *tithi*-s found in the old edition have been corrected. In the old edition, the variant and difficult Chinese characters had not been examined thoroughly. In this new edition, I have taken into consideration readings from the old manuscripts and, as much as possible, I have used the characters I consider closest to the original.

(5) Records of Sunday Brought to Japan from China by Kūkai

On p.102, I wrote that on the last folio in the colophon of the Kakushō edition, Kakushō listed all the first Sundays of the first month for three years, starting from the twenty-fifth year of Enryaku 延暦. Concerning this point, I would like to make some additional remarks. In the Muryōjuin manuscript of Kōyasan (mentioned earlier in the "Additional Remarks" on the First Chapter), the first Sundays of the twenty-fifth year of Enryaku (first year of Daidō) and the second year of Daidō were mentioned in the manuscript. This manuscript (label no.125) was divided into first and second fascicles. Nothing was mentioned about the

[65] For those mentioned in the *Qiyao rangzai jue*, please refer to the chart on Yano 2004:142.

third year of Daidō. This is the case also for the Jimyōin manuscript. However, in the Muryōjuin manuscript (label no.124) in one "complete fascicle," as well in the Doshisha manuscript, these descriptions of Sundays are not to be found at all. It thus becomes clear to me that the Muryōjuin manuscript seen by Kakushō was the manuscript label no.125. Moreover, from Kakushō's description of the third Sunday, that is, the third year of Daidō, I believe that such a description may have been found in the Hakkōin manuscript. Unfortunately, the whereabouts of the Hakkōin manuscript is unknown. Kakushō had probably collated all the three dates from the different manuscripts in the edition and noted that oddity of third "second month." As a result, he put a special mark (O) beside the character "second" 二 in the text and made a correction to the date in the apparatus in the header.

Concerning the combination of the weekdays and the twenty-seven lunar mansions, Yamashita Katsuaki had pointed out that even a hundred years before Fujiwara no Michinaga, his great grandfather Fujiwara no Tadahira 藤原忠平 had already mentioned them in his diary *Teishinkōki* 貞信公記. Furthermore, special days such as the Amṛta Day and the Rakṣas Day are also indicated.

IV. THE JAPANESE EDITION OF THE *XIUYAO JING*

1. The Day of the Week of the New Moon Day of the Second Month of the Sixteenth Year of Kyōhō (1731 CE)

After I realized that the Kakushō edition of the *Xiuyao jing* was far superior to the Continental edition and contained readings much closer to the original, I was keen to see for myself the manuscripts used for this edition. According to Morita, the oldest manuscripts are the ones kept in Kanchiin 観智院 of Tōji and another one in Muryōjuin of Kōyasan. I then made a visit to these two temples. In July 1985, I had the good fortune to join the research group led by Prof. Uejima Tamotsu 上島有 of Setsunan University 摂南大学 and saw the first and second fascicles of the Tōji manuscript of the *Xiuyao jing*. While the second fascicle appeared to be quite new judging by the paper quality, the first fascicle could be dated back as far as the Nanbokuchō 南北朝 period (14th century).

At the end of October of the same year, I made a trip to Kōyasan. As I was planning to give a talk on the *Xiuyao jing* at a conference held in India later in the middle of November, I wanted to see as many manuscripts as possible beforehand. Prior to the visit, a list of manuscripts available at Kōyasan University related to the *Xiuyao jing* was helpfully prepared by Muroji Yoshihito 室寺義仁, who was formerly of Kōyasan University and was then a teaching assistant in the Faculty of Letters of Kyoto University.

The manuscript in the Muryōjuin collection that was supposedly used by Kakushō in his edition was at that time kept in the Reihōkan Museum 靈寶館 at Kōyasan. Regrettably I had no chance to see it. I was, however, able to examine the next oldest manuscript, namely, the Jimyōin 持明院 manuscript dated the third year of *Katei* 嘉禎 (1237 CE), which was deposited at the Kōyasan University Library. As I had expected, it was similar to the Tōji manuscript, and I could confirm that Kakushō indeed used this manuscript in his edition.

Among the old texts that I had access to in the same library, what I found most interesting was the *Xiuyao jing suanyaozhi zhang diqi quan* 宿曜經算曜直章第七全, a manuscript also from Jimyōin that had been temporarily deposited at the Kōyasan University Library. As previously mentioned, one of the purposes of my investigation was to confirm with my own eyes whether the chapter Yang Jingfeng added to the *Xiuyao jing* could actually be found among the old Japanese manuscripts, thus I had been looking forward to seeing it since I saw the title in Muroji's list. As its title suggests, this manuscript in Japanese binding was composed to explain only the contents of the Seventh Section. Detailed comments were added along the original text of the Seventh Section, excerpted in its original order. The author explained carefully the computational technique for the calculation of weekdays and the sexagenary dates, by taking the example of the new moon day of the second month of the sixteenth year of *Kyōhō* 享保. According to the text, the inclusive sum of years from the Epoch (*Shangyuan* 上元) of the "Suanyaozhi zhang" to that day is 2518. To be precise, this number corresponds to the sum of years from the Epoch, or in other words, it is the variable Y on p.100. For the other values, $m = 0$ and $t = 1$, since this day was the "new moon of the second month." If one uses the four formulae on p.100, the values A (the sum of intercalary months), M (the sum of months), U (the sum of omitted civil days) and D (the sum of civil days) can be easily calculated. In fact, applying the algorithm, the author of this manual obtained the result of 919672 for the sum of days since the Epoch. This result is correct mathematically. If one divides this number by seven, the remainder is five. As previously mentioned, since the Epoch of the "Suanyaozhi zhang" was taken to be a Monday, the remainder of five would correspond to a Friday. If one takes the same sum of days from the Epoch and divides it by sixty, the remainder is fifty-two. As the Epoch was thought to be a *Jiachen* 甲辰, the reminder fifty-two would become *Yiwei* 乙未. Thus this author made the new moon day of the second month of the sixteenth year of *Kyōhō* to be Friday and *Yiwei*.

However, the new moon day of the second month of the sixteenth year of *Kyōhō*—that is, 8 March 1731 CE—was in fact Thursday and *Jiawu* 甲午, not Friday and *Yiwei* as the author of this text claimed. In other words, the day the author obtained was the second, rather than the first day of the second month. He was off by one day because the Epoch had been placed too far away.

Unfortunately, the name of the author of this strange manual is unknown. He had probably realized that the algorithm from this Seventh

Section was not good enough. Nevertheless, he retained this part of the text without discarding it probably to try to save the "face" of this prestigious sūtra. Judging from the years of the sample calculation, this person could be none other than Kakushō.

The calendrical techniques found in sixth-century Indian astronomical works were incorporated into Esoteric Buddhist astrological works in eighth century China without being completely understood. They were then transmitted verbatim to Japan, and subsequently monks continued to struggle with them almost a thousand years later. In Japan, located at the periphery of the transmission, there was no way for one to know that these techniques had already been rendered useless in their place of origin.

2. The Roles of the First and Second Fascicles of the *Xiuyao jing*

I have so far covered all the contents of the *Xiuyao jing*, as edited and annotated by Yang Jingfeng under Amoghavajra's supervision. Meanwhile, the explanation of Shi Yao's first translation, i.e., the second fascicle of the *Xiuyao jing*, has also more or less come to an end. There is one topic, however, discussed in the second fascicle but not recapitulated in the first fascicle. This is the so-called "Techniques on Prohibited Movements" *Xingdong jinbi fa* 行動禁閉法, in which the auspiciousness or inauspiciousness of the cardinal directions is described, based on which of the twenty-seven *nakṣatra*-s or twelve zodiacal signs each day "belongs to." Since the way a day "belongs to" a *nakṣatra* or a zodiacal sign has not been defined in the text, this method cannot be applied. Moreover, we cannot reconstruct this method from the Indian sources. Yang Jingfeng must have deleted this section realizing that he could not use it.

For ordinary Chinese readers, it would have been fine if there were only the newer, retranslated first fascicle. However, it was customary for Buddhists to treat both old and new translations with reverence. In fact, one often may gain a better understanding of the text if one refers to the old translation while reading the new one. If one considers the first and second fascicles of the *Xiuyao jing* as new and old translations in this manner, one may understand how the two fascicles came to be combined into one despite their large amount of overlapping material. In fact, I myself have also gained a better understanding of the text by comparing the two.

As far as scientific texts are concerned, new ones inevitably replace the old ones once they become obsolete and forgotten. But the *Xiuyao jing* is not a purely scientific text in this sense. Rather, precisely because astrology was a kind of knowledge that went beyond the level of science, Amoghavajra tried to use these new techniques from India to promote Esoteric Buddhism as the state religion of China. Although he had once instructed his disciple to translate the text, five years later he asked a lay disciple to retranslate it under his personal supervision. Amoghavajra must have been much concerned with the success of this "sūtra."

However, astronomy and calendars had a long history in China and the *Xiuyao jing* did not exert an influence on China to the degree Amoghavajra had hoped for. On the other hand, the astrological school of *Sukuyōdō* formed in Japan, and it took this text as the basis of its teaching and has endured all the way up to the twentieth century. After periods of decline during the Muromachi and Edo Periods, some elements of *Sukuyōdō* were revived as is reflected in modern Japanese almanacs.

3. From *Xiuyao jing* to Sukuyōdō

Both Ennin 円仁 and Enchin 円珍 brought the same text back from China as had Kūkai before them, but as the previous discussion should have made clear, it is not necessarily the case that these later versions are any better than the previous one.

What is transmitted in the *Xiuyao jing* is only the very basics of Indian astrology. While Indian astrology may be divided into a number of fields, the content of the *Xiuyao jing* is the closest to what is called a "*muhūrta*" text. Muhūrta is an Indian unit of time equivalent to a thirtieth of a day. As a general term, it just means "time," and specifically, auspicious or inauspicious times. The "auspicious and inauspicious time and days" (*jixiong shiri* 吉凶時日) in the long title of the *Xiuyao jing* refers to this concept, also known as catarchic astrology.[66]

A *muhūrta* text is a collection of omens or divination from ancient India. While its main theme concerns the relation between the Moon and the *nakṣatra*-s, such a text often includes portents based on natural phenomena such as meteors, comets, halos around the Sun, rainbows or thunder, extending as well to a broad range of mantic arts such as bird divination, oneiromancy and physiognomy. Some of the representative texts featuring materials from this ancient period are the *Śārdūlakarṇāvadāna* and the *Atharvavedapariśiṣṭa*, while the *Gargasaṃhitā* and the *Bṛhatsaṃhitā* include newer material. As such, the *Xiuyao jing* shares many similarities with these texts.

On the other hand, the genethlical astrology that was transmitted from the West spread to India in a short period of time, creating a new subgenre known as *jātaka*. Since this new field of astrology required the calculation of planetary positions, the Indian mathematical astronomy that accompanied it flourished as well.[67] Beside the calculation of

[66] Pingree 1981:101.

[67] Although Buddha's past lives stories are called *jātaka*, as a genre of astrological texts, it means "divination based on birth," i.e., genethlical astrology or horoscopy.

planetary positions, the tools and methods for divination also had become more complicated and specialized.

Therefore, when Amoghavajra made his visit to south India and Ceylon in the middle of the eighth century, Indian astrology must have been very specialized. However, such specialized techniques are not found in his *Xiuyao jing*. As far as new material is concerned, there is just mere mention of concepts such as the seven luminaries, the twelve zodiacal signs and the Twelve Places. In India, the astrologers maintain their authority as professionals through a combination of complicated astronomical calculations of planetary positions and complex teachings of divination. One wonders whether Amoghavajra thought that he could nonetheless make the *Xiuyao jing* a success without incorporating such advanced techniques into the text. Or could it be simply that Amoghavajra did not have the chance to acquire such professional knowledge?

The *Xiuyao jing* transmitted to Japan enabled the making of a kind of divination different from that of the "Yin-Yang School" (Ch. Yinyangdao, Jp. Onmyōdō 陰陽道), which originated in China. However, it was impossible to challenge *Onmyōdō* with only the material in this text. The monks who went to China after Kūkai must have felt the need to look for more specialized astrological texts. In the following chapter, I will discuss a few texts that can be considered to have contributed to making the *Xiuyao jing* the fundamental text of *Sukuyōdō*.

Chapter Four—Additional Notes

In the example calculation, the author of the *Xiuyao jing suanyaozhi zhang diqi quan* 宿曜經算曜直章第七全 of the Kōyasan manuscript obtained a result of Friday, *Yiwei*, for the weekday and sexagenary date of the first day of the second month of sixteenth year of Kyōhō. However, I wonder whether the author of this manual knew that the result was wrong. If he knew that the method in Section Seven was useless, he might not have left such a detailed example of the computation. At any rate, while I have not made any amendment to my old edition, I would like to propose a solution. If the first month of that year had been a big month instead of a small month, the result from the calculation would be correct. Although unexpected, the author of the manuscript may have also thought of this solution.

The author of this Kōyasan manuscript had understood well the relationship between the first and second fascicle of the *Xiuyao jing*. He pointed out that although the two translations were described separately at the beginning as the "Shi Yao version" and the "Yang Jingfeng version," at some point, the "Shi Yao version" became the first fascicle and the "Yang Jingfeng version" became the second fascicle. He suggested that at the end, the "Yang Jingfeng version" came to be called the first fascicle and the "Shi Yao version" the second.

In the quotation from the "Suanyaozhi zhang," the author also points out the correct reading of "three" 三 instead of "four" 四, which I mentioned above.

V. DEVELOPMENT OF SUKUYŌDŌ IN JAPAN

1. Ptolemy and *Duliyusi jing* 都利聿斯經

In the *Shin shosha shōrai hōmontō mokuroku* 新書寫請來法門等目錄, Taishō (2174A), the catalogue of texts brought back to Japan by Shūei 宗叡, a monk from Tōji, in the seventh year of Jōgan 貞觀 (865), ten titles are listed under "miscellaneous works." These works are described as texts that "people may need, though they do not belong to Buddhism." The following four out of ten are related to astrology:

i) *Duliyusi jing* 都利聿斯經, one item in five fascicles
ii) *Qiyao rangzai jue* 七曜禳災決, in one fascicle
iii) *Qiyao ershibaxiu li* 七曜二十八宿曆, in one fascicle
iv) *Qiyao liri* 七曜曆日, in one fascicle

Among these, the *Qiyao rangzai jue* 七曜禳災決[68] will be discussed later. As for the remaining three, the titles of the last two suggest both their nature and that they might belong to the same category as the *Xiuyao jing*. Unfortunately, the two texts are no longer extant.

The *Duliyusi jing*, which also appears as a title in the Chinese historical records, is no longer extant in either China or Japan. As was first pointed out by Dr. Ishida Mikinosuke, however, the text appears to have been well read by the Japanese *Sukuyōdō* astrologers. It was quoted frequently with the words "according to *Yusi jing*" in the *Sukuyō kanmon* 宿曜勘文, a genre of texts from the Heian period which give explanations of horoscopes. Dr. Ishida points out that the title "*Duliyusi jing*, two fascicles," together with "*Yusi simen jing* 聿斯四門經, one fascicle" are found in the *Yiwenzhi* 藝文志 ("Treatise on Literature") of the *Xintangshu* 新唐書 ("New Tang History"), and that the latter work *Yusi simen jing* was abbreviated as *Simen jing* (lit. Four-door Sūtra). Moreover, he shows that the title *Simen jing* is found in the catalogue of sūtras brought to the Tang court by the Nestorian monk Jingjing 景淨, known also as Adam. Ishida's conclusion is that since both the *Simen*

[68] 禳 reads also 攘.

jing and the *Duliyusi jing* have their origin in India, they must have entered China through Central Asia.[69]

On the other hand, Prof. Yabuuti, examining the fragments of the *Yusi jing* cited in the Japanese *Sukuyō kanmon* discovered by Ishida, had the opinion that the text was based on Greek instead of Indian astrology. In particular, the name *Simen jing*, literally Sūtra of Four Gates, seems to suggest that it may have some kind of connections with Ptolemy's *Tetrabiblos*.[70]

The Greek title of Ptolemy's astrological text was purportedly *Apotelesmatika*. In Latin, it is commonly called *Tetrabiblos* (Book of Four Parts) since it contains four books. It was also translated into Arabic as *Kitāb al-arba' al-maqālāt* ("The Four-Part Book"). It is of no surprise that the text would have been called the "Sūtra of Four Gates" in Chinese.[71]

As for "Duliyusi," many have suggested that the word should be analyzed as "Duli" and "Yusi," making the first part a place name while the latter a personal name. Recently, an essay was written to prove that "Duli" was the Talas River, where China and Islam first confronted each other. However, as I have tried to move forward with Prof. Yabuuti's explanation concerning the *Simen jing*, I have come to the conclusion that "Duliyusi" is most likely the name Ptolemy. Ptolemy's *Tetrabiblos* was circulated so widely to the extent that it was called the "Bible of Astrology." Since it was translated into Syriac in the seventh century and into Persian toward the end of the eighth century, it is not inconceivable that it was also known in Tang China.

The Nestorian Christians are said to be largely responsible for bringing Greek sciences to the East. The inscription *Daqin jingjiao liuxing zhongguo bei* 大秦景教流行中國碑, dated 781 CE, shows how Nestorianism had reached Tang China and flourished to the extent that a temple called *Daqin si* 大秦寺 ("Roman Temple") was built in the capital Chang'an. It is highly possible that the presentation of the "Sūtra of Four Gates" or *Simen jing* by Adam (*Jingjing*) to the court of Tang and a translation from the Syriac or Persian edition of the *Tetrabiblos* were at around the same time.

In written Syriac, just as in Pahlavi, vowels are not shown. It would have been customary for a Greek name like Ptolemy to be written in

[69] Ishida 1950:49–62.
[70] Yabuuti 1969:186–91.
[71] Yano 1990:219.

consonants only, as P-T-L-M-Y-V-S. The first letter P is easily dropped (as in the English pronunciation). And if for whatever reason the M is dropped, too, it would have become T (*du* 都) L (*li* 利) YV (*yu* 聿) S (*si* 斯). Therefore, (*Duli*) *yusi simen jing* might actually have been "Ptolemy's *Tetrabiblos*." As I expect a debate on the matter, I would like to present the idea here as a hypothesis.

Since Ptolemy was a master of ancient scholarship including not only astronomy and geography, but also astrology, many spurious works have been attributed to him: therefore, one cannot assert with complete confidence that the *Duliyusi jing* brought back to Japan by the monk Shūei was the Chinese translation of Ptolemy's *Tetrabiblos*. From an examination of the extant passages in citation, however, it is certain that the *Duliyusi jing* is based on the genethliacal astrology of Western origin.

For example, in a passage cited in the *Kanmon* as "according to the *Yusi jing*," the term "*sanhe*" 三合 (of two planets) often appears. This is one of the aspects (spatial relationship among planets) in Western astrology called the *trine*, or in other words, a relationship when planets are separated by 120°. While the concept of "aspect" is one of the basic elements of genethliacal astrology, it is not mentioned in the *Xiuyao jing*.

Ishida reported that references to the *Yusi jing* can be found in the *Xiuyao jing*, but this is probably not the case. However, the expression "according to the *Yusi jing*" 聿斯經 is found in a text called *Fantian huoluo jiuyao* 梵天火羅九曜 (Taishō 1311). Since the text contains a passage that relates to *Rāhu* and *Ketu*, which we will discuss later, it cannot come from the *Tetrabiblos* at all.

With Shūei's introduction of the *Duliyisi jing* to Japan, it became possible to practically "read" a horoscope with the interpretation given in the text. What still remained were methods for the correct calculation of the planetary positions and the preparation of the horoscope. Although later an excellent calendar known as *Futian li* 符天曆 was introduced, until then, it was the *Qiyao rangzai jue* brought by Shūei that played an important role in obtaining the planetary positions.

2. Planetary Ephemerides: The Role of the *Qiyao rangzai jue* 七曜攘災决

The *Qiyao rangzai jue* brought to Japan by Shūei is thankfully preserved in Japan in its entirety.[72] As this text has not been preserved in any of the Tripiṭaka-s in China, the Taishō edition of this text is based only on a sole manuscript from Hasedera Temple 長谷寺 copied in the second year of Kyōwa 享和 (1802 CE) without variant readings from other manuscripts. According to a note at the end of this Taishō edition, it was the monk Kaidō 快道 of Hasedera who edited the text based on a manuscript from the Ninnaji 仁和寺 collection. As I was interested in the positions of planets which comprise a large part of the *Qiyao rangzai jue*, I had always wanted to make a detailed analysis of the text. However, since the text in the Taishō Tripiṭaka had a number of editorial errors just as in the case of the *Xiuyao jing*, I felt the strong need to examine the original manuscript. I tried to locate them in Hasedera and Ninnaji by writing to the temples, but unfortunately, both temples replied to me that the manuscripts could not be located.

With no other choice, I began working with the Taishō edition and made an interesting discovery which I shall explain below.

In July, 1985, I came to learn about a manuscript of the *Qiyao rangzai jue* mentioned in an essay by Momo Hiroyuki 桃裕行. After sending him a letter, I rather unexpectedly received photos of the manuscript from the professor, taken from a manuscript he knew of in an antiquarian bookstore in Tokyo. However, the manuscript itself was sold soon afterwards and its location is presently unknown. The following is written in the colophon of the text, based on the manuscript's photo:

[72] Taishō(1308)21.

保安三年九月一日摂洲八部郡法隆寺須磨庄以木花木筆書之生年卌歳也

永久四年四年三月七日伝授之珎也

日本第百十九之宿曜師

珎也之本

Written on the first day of the ninth month of the third year of Hōan (1122) at Suma-shō of Hōryūji, Yatabe-gun, Sesshū. Aged forty.

[By] Chinya, received on the seventh day of the third month of the fourth year of Eikyū

The 119th [generation] Sukuyōshi astrologer of Japan

The text of Chinya

This manuscript was copied at the end of the Heian period—in other words, at the time when Sukuyōdō was at its peak.

The manuscript was worm-eaten and some parts remain unreadable. Nonetheless, since it was at least copied by someone who understood its contents, unlike the text made by the editors of the Taishō Tripiṭaka, the information it provides is extremely valuable. While I would like to make an analysis of the ephemerides based on this manuscript as soon as possible, in this book I would like to discuss at least the role of this text in Sukuyōdō.[73]

According to the *Qiyao rangzai jue*, this book was "composed by a Brahmin priest called 'Jinjutuo' 金俱吒 of Western India 西天竺." It is not clear what area "Western India" actually refers to or what the Sanskrit name of the Brahman monk "Jinjutuo" would have been. However, judging from its contents, it is unlikely that the text actually has a Sanskrit source. Although the topics involve astrological material transmitted from the West, such as the seven luminaries, the twelve zodiacal signs and the Twelve Places, its astronomical content is closer to the Chinese system than the Indian one. It may be described as an amalgamation of Indian astrology and Chinese astronomy. Judging from the ephemerides in this text, the work was composed some time between the end of the eighth century and the beginning of the ninth. This text would have been unknown to Kūkai as it was Shūei who first brought it to Japan.

[73] Yano 1986:28–35; Yano 1995:73–81.

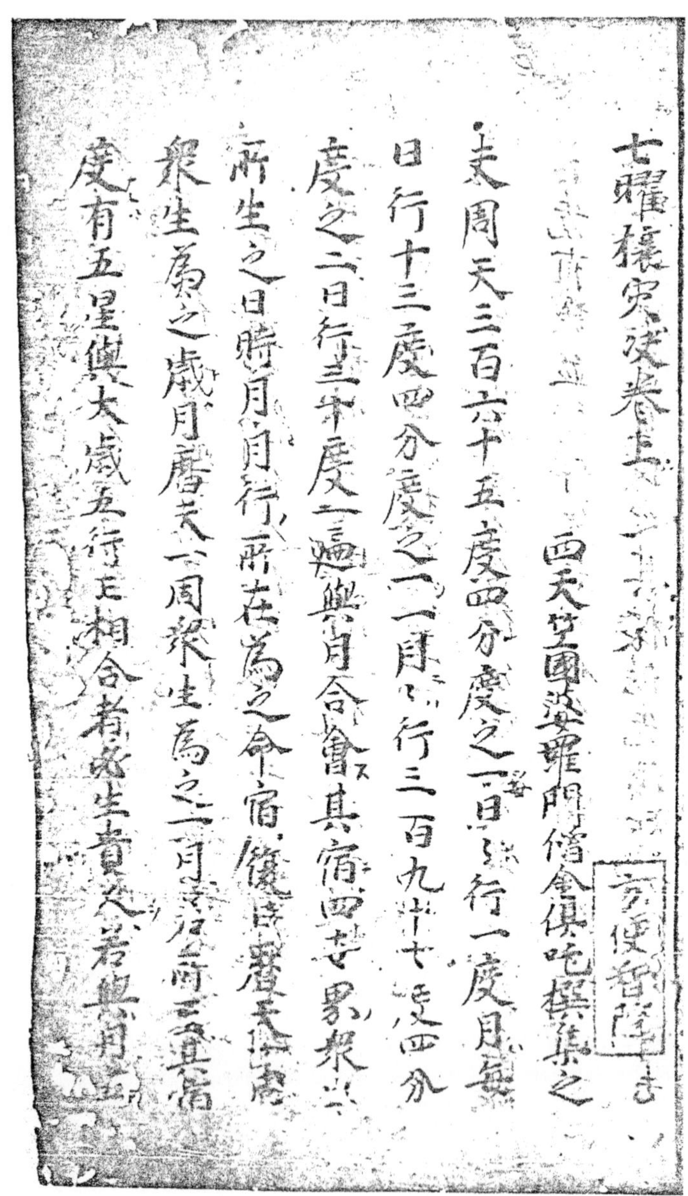
七曜攘災決卷上
西天竺國婆羅門僧金俱吒撰集之
方便智院
夫周天三百六十五度四分度之一日行一度月每
日行十三度四分度之一月行三百九十七度四分
度之二日行三十度一遍與月合會其宿四廿累衆生
所生之日時月月行所在為之命宿復推曆天係宿
衆生為之歲月曆天下周衆生為之二月以所三宜宿
度有五星與太歲五行王相合者必生貴人若與月至

Fig.38 First folio of a Japanese manuscript of *Qiyao Rangzai jue*.

The Seven Luminaries 七曜 and the Nine *Graha*-s 九執

Rangzaijue 攘災决 refers to the method of preventing various disasters, which are believed to be caused by the planets.[74] Although "seven luminaries" are mentioned in the title of the *Qiyao rangzai jue*, the two pseudo-planets Rāhu and Ketu are also discussed. The Chinese terms *luohou* (Jap. *rago*) 羅睺 and *jidu* (Jap. *keito*) 計都 are simply phonetic transcriptions of Sanskrit *Rāhu* and *Ketu* respectively. In Indian astronomy/astrology, these two invisible planets are added to the seven luminaries to make up the *navagraha*. As *nava* and *graha* mean "nine" and "seizer" respectively, the term was translated as *jiuzhi* 九執 in Chinese. The *Jiuzhi li* 九執曆, a work on astronomical calculation that was mentioned earlier, carries the same term in its title. In India, even today, there is the belief that the nine *graha*-s "seize" people and bring about disaster.

Fig.39 ***Navagraha*-s**

(© W. Hartner. *Oriens Occidens*)

[74] Yano 2001:274–75.

Fig.40 ***Navagraha*-s in Kapaleśvara monastery, Madras.**

(© Photo by Michio Yano)

While it may sound strange that a text with a title of "seven luminaries" discusses the "nine *graha*-s," the text in fact begins with a section titled "Techniques of predicting and preventing disasters" 占災攘之法, in which only the Sun, the Moon and the five planets are mentioned. These techniques of disaster prevention involving the seven luminaries contain many Chinese elements: for example, the order of the five planets which is identical to the Chinese Five Phases 五行.

The Measurement of Lunar Mansions in Degrees

Under the heading of "The Measurement of Lunar Mansions in Degrees" (*Xiudufa* 宿度法), the twenty-eight lunar mansions are divided in the following manner:[75]

[75] °° indicat Chinese degrees. Numbers in brackets identify the twenty-seven lunar mansions (see Fig.23). One revolution consists of $365\frac{1}{4}$°° (Chinese degree). 1°° = 0.98564° (Yano 1986:31, 34 fn.10).

East 75°°	角 (14) 亢 (15) 氐 (16) 房 (17) 心 (18) 尾 (19) 箕 (20)
North 98°°	斗 (21) 牛[76] 女 (22) 虚 (23) 危 (24) 室 (25) 壁 (26)
West 80°°	奎 (27) 婁 (1) 胃 (2) 昴 (3) 畢 (4) 觜 (5) 参 (6)
South 113°°	井 (7) 鬼 (8) 柳 (9) 星 (10) 張 (11) 翼 (12) 軫 (13)

The lunar mansions above add up to 366°° in Chinese degrees. In Chinese astronomy, the number of degrees in the celestial sphere are based on the number of days in a solar year. Therefore, while the length may vary slightly according to the calendrical canon, the number of degrees in the celestial sphere is always a little bit more than 365. The size of the Chinese degree is thus smaller than the Western degree.

The twenty-eight lunar mansions are divided into groups of seven starting from *Jiao* 角 (= *Citrā*). The way these groups are made to correspond to the four cardinal directions is typically Chinese. However, I do not know of another almanacal work from China in which the width of the lunar mansions of the four directions (as measured on the equator or the ecliptic) are given the same values as above. Such values cannot be found in the astronomical sections of any of the official histories. The closest example would be that of the equatorial degrees of the lunar lodges found in the Treatise on Astronomy (*Lüli zhi* 律曆志) of the *Xuhan shu* 續漢書, which add up to a total of $365\frac{1}{4}$°°:

Eastern lodges: 75°°
Northern lodges: $98\frac{1}{4}$°°
Western lodges: 80°°
Southern lodges: 112°°

Seven Luminaries and Twelve Places

In the section titled the "Table of Seven Luminaries" *Qiyao bangtong* 七曜旁通, the auspiciousness and inauspiciousness of combinations of the Twelve Places and the seven luminaries are shown in a table. Although the label "Twelve Signs" 十二宮 is used in the text, the text uses the names of the Twelve Places (as is shown in Fig.21). In other words, Western genethliacal astrology has obviously been taken as the premise of the work. This table shows whether it is auspicious or

[76] *Abhijit* not included in the twenty-seven *nakṣatra*-system.

inauspicious when one of the seven luminaries enters into each of the places from the first to the twelfth (arranged as shown in Fig.20). Below this table there is a short section titled *Jiuzhi zhi xingnian fa* 九執至行年法, the contents of which are not entirely clear.[77]

Next, the text describes the auspiciousness and inauspiciousness of the entry of the Sun and the Moon into each of the Twelve Places. In particular, the text gives a visual correspondence between the parts of the human body and the twenty-eight *nakṣatra*-s (Fig.34), and mentions also alternative methods of determining an individual's *nakṣatra* in case the person himself does not know.[78] After this section, mantras corresponding to each of the nine luminaries are given.

Planetary Ephemerides[79]

What I have described above is the introductory part of the "disaster-preventing" features of the *Qiyao rangzai jue*. From this point onward, the text moves on to the topic of the calculation of planetary positions, a subject of great interest from the viewpoint of the history of astronomy. As mentioned previously, the *Xiuyao jing* offers only a basic knowledge of Indian astrology: it would not have been possible to practice specialized arts of astrology with only that text. The most essential element, missing from the *Xiuyao jing*, would be the calculation of planetary positions; and even the *Jiuzhi li*, which is of Indian origin, does not include this material for the five planets. The *Qiyao rangzai jue*, however, gives the planetary positions in the form of a table, providing the calculated values.

In the *Qiyao rangzai jue*, eight ephemerides are given in total: in order, Jupiter, Mars, Saturn, Venus, Mercury, Rāhu, Ketu and the Sun. The ephemeris for the Moon is not provided. Each ephemeris, except that of the Sun, is preceded by a brief list of astronomical constants, such as the mean motion and other planetary phenomena.[80] The astronomical constants for the Sun are treated separately at the end. Comparing the average planetary motion in the *Qiyao rangzai jue* with those of various Chinese astronomical texts of the Tang Period,

---

[77] The content is a summary of the astrological text *Fantian huoluo jiuyao* 梵天火羅九曜 (Taishō No.1311) translated by Yixing 一行. Another summary is found in the Tōji *Horā Scroll* (See front piece of Yano 1994).

[78] Yano 1992:39, 121–24.

[79] For detailed explanation on this topic, see Yano 1986.

[80] For the planetary phenomena, see Neugebauer 1975:386.

Prof. Yabuuti shows that in terms of the material, the *Qiyao rangzai jue* is closest to the *Wuji li* 五紀曆.[81] Fig.41 is a comparison of the motion of Jupiter according to the *Qiyao rangzai jue* and other Chinese astronomical texts cited from the work of Prof. Yabuuti.

Astronomical work	*Qiyao rangzai jue*	Linde 麟德	Dayan 大衍	Wuji 五紀	Zhengyuan 正元
Synodic Period: *Zhongri* 終日 (days)	399	398.86	398.87	398.88	398.90
Progression after first appearance: *Chuchenjian shunxing* 初晨見順行	114	114	112	114	114
First station: *Liu* 留	27	26	27	27	26
Retrogradation: *Tui* 退	82.5	84	86	82	84
Second station: *Liu* 留	27	25	27	27	25
Progression: *Shunxing* 順行	114	114	112	114	114
Disappearnace: *Fu* 伏	34	35.86	34.87	34.88	35.9

Fig.41 Comparison of the motion of Jupiter according to *Qiyao rangzai jue* and other Chinese astronomical works.

Here the "complete [cycle in] days" (*zhongri* 終日) is equivalent to Jupiter's synodic period. In other words, this value is the period starting from Jupiter's first appearance in the morning in the eastern sky (in progressive motion), after its conjunction with the Sun. Then after the first stationary position (*liu* 留), it moves in retrograde motion. After the second stationary position, Jupiter then moves in progressive motion again. The planet disappears (*fu* 伏) as it approaches the Sun again, until the next first appearance in the morning (in progressive motion). Since

[81] Calendar used during the Tang Period from 762 to 783 CE.

the synodic period of Jupiter is around 399 days, a repetition of 76 periods would be $399 \times 76 = 30{,}324$ days. This is equivalent to approximately 83 years. During this time, Jupiter would have made seven sidereal rotations—the difference between the 83 completions of the Sun's sidereal rotation and the 76 conjunctions of the Sun and Jupiter in this period. Once this 83-year cycle table for the motion of Jupiter is prepared, it could be used for subsequent cycles as roughly the same motions would be repeated. Each year is divided into twelve parts, each labeled with the month from the first to the twelfth. The position of Jupiter on the first day of each month is given by the coordinates of the twenty-eight lunar lodges. The same principles apply to the other four planets—in a certain rounded up number of years, in a certain rounded up number of revolutions, a planet conjoins with the Sun and during that time the planet would revolve over the sidereal sphere for a certain rounded up number of times, as expressed in Fig.42. It may be noted that the number of sidereal rotations of Venus and Mercury is same as the number of rotations (in years) of the Sun.

The values of the six lower rows add up to the value of synodic period in the top row. However, the figures in the *Qiyao rangzai jue* are rounded up.

	Number of years	Number of conjunctions	Number of revolutions
Jupiter	83	76	7
Mars	79	37	42
Saturn	59	57	2
Venus	8	5	8
Mercury	33	104	33

Fig.42 Periodicity of Planets.

Since the tenth year of Zhengyuan 貞元 (794 CE) is adopted as the first year of the table of positions for the five planets—that is, as the Epoch—one may consider the *Qiyao rangzai jue* to have been composed at around that time.

As previously mentioned, the planetary positions in the table are given at the beginning of every month from the first to the twelfth. It should however be explained what this "month" actually refers to. If this "month" were the synodic month, then a twelve month period would consist of 354 days (29.5×12): this is not suitable for use as a

八十三年	·········	三年	二年	一年	年数／月
十九退井三十	·········	三日留氐一	退	退張	正月
留井	·········	退亢	退軫	廿二退留張八	二月
順鬼柳	·········	亢	廿二退軫一	留張	三月
柳	·········	廿一日亢初	留	留張	四月
柳	·········	守亢	留	張	五月
七日伏星二	·········	守亢	留	翼	六月
十日見張初	·········	亢	留	九日伏翼八度	七月
張	·········	氐	十日伏軫卜九	十二日見翼十二	八月
張	·········	九日伏氐八	十日見角	翼	九月
張	·········	十二見氐十三	角	軫	十月
三日留張十九	·········	房	亢	軫	十一月
退張	·········	心	亢	四日留軫十二	十二月

Fig.43 Jupiter's ephemeris[82]

time reference system, as it is eleven days shorter than the solar year. On the other hand, if a month is defined as one-twelfth of a solar year, twelve months could suitably function as a reference for time. In fact, the "month" used here is just this kind of a month, equivalent to something called *saura-māsa* ("solar month") in India.

One-twelfth of one solar year corresponds to 30° (or one zodiacal sign) of the movement of the Sun. This division is based on the Sun's

[82] See original in Fig.53 (p.153).

entry (*saṃkrānti*) into each zodiacal sign. A year is divided in this manner, and the intercalary months are then inserted. This idea is just the same as dividing one synodic month into thirty equal parts and thereafter one determines the omitted days and decide whether the month is "big" (30 days) or "small" (29 days). The twenty-four "solar terms" (*jieqi* 節氣),[83] play the same role in Chinese astronomy.

The table of planetary positions are given by the coordinates of the twenty-eight lunar lodges. In Fig.43, the first three and the last (83rd) columns of the table for Jupiter are taken as an example.

According to this table, Jupiter is in the lodge *Zhang* 張 in the first month of the first year and in retrograde motion (*tui* 退). It continues to be in retrograde motion until the twenty-second day of the second month. Afterward, at 8°° of *Zhang*, it reaches the "second" stationary position (*liu* 留). After remaining in this stationary position in the third and fourth months, it moves in progressive motion in the fifth and sixth months. On the ninth day of the seventh month, Jupiter approaches the Sun and becomes invisible (*fu* 伏) at 8°° of *Yi* 翼. On the eleventh day of the eighth month, it becomes visible again at 12°° of *Yi*. The planet continues to move in progressive motion until the fourth day of the twelfth month when it reaches the "first" stationary position at 12°° of *Zhen* 軫 (Figs.44, 53).

In this way the motion of Jupiter during eighty-three years is tabulated. Only eight-three years are needed because in the eighty-fourth year Jupiter returns to the same pattern as the first year. Since the synodic period is not particularly precise, after the repetition of two or three cycles there would naturally be a slight sidereal misalignment.

In such a way, the monthly positions of the five planets are tabulated for the respective synodic period (Fig.42). This kind of table is called an ephemeris (pl. ephemerides). To analyze these ephemerides from an astronomical point of view, one must first establish the coordinates that are represented by the twenty-eight lodges. Chinese astronomical works usually use two coordinate systems (equatorial lodge degree 赤道宿度 and ecliptic lodge degree 黄道宿度) and give the degrees between the determinative stars (*juxing* 距星) of the two lodges; however, the *Qiyao rangzai jue* gives only the width of four groups of seven lodges as shown in p.127. Luckily, the daily motion of the Sun is tabulated at the

[83] A seasonal unit which is based on the movement of the Sun, dividing one solar year into twenty-four equal parts.

end of the text. This enables us to reconstruct the coordinates of the twenty-eight lodges. In Fig.44, I have prepared a table giving the result of this attempt together with the values from the *Dayan li* 大衍曆, a representative work among the Tang calendars.

Lunar Lodge		Determinative star	*Dayan li*	*Qiyao rangzai jue*
1	Kui 奎	ζ And	17½	17
2	Lou 婁	β Ari	12¾	13
3	Wei 胃	35 Ari	14¾	14
4	Mao 昴	η Tau	11	11
5	Bibu 畢	ε Tau	16¼	16
6	Zui 觜	λ Ori	1	1
7	Shen 參	δ Ori	9¼	10
8	Jing 井	μ Gem	30	30
9	Gui 鬼	θ Cnc	2¾	3
10	Liu 柳	δ Hya	14¼	14
11	Xing 星	α Hya	6¾	7
12	Zhang 張	υ Hya	18¾	19
13	Yi 翼	α Crt	19¼	19
14	Zhen 軫	γ Crv	18¾	19
15	Jiao 角	α Vir	13	13
16	Kang 亢	χ Vir	9	9
17	Di 氐	α Lib	1 5 ṛ	16
18	Fang 房	π Sco	5	5
19	Xin 心	σ Sco	4¾	5
20	Wei 尾	Sco	17	17
21	Ji 箕	γ Sgr	10¼	10
22	Dou 斗	φ Sgr	23½	23
23	Niu 牛	β Cap	7½	8
24	Nü 女	ε Aqr	11¼	11
25	Xu 虛	β Aqr	$10^{90}/_{3040}$	10
26	Wei 危	α Aqr	17¾	18
27	Shi 室	α Peg	17¼	17
28	Bi 壁	γ Peg	9¾	10

Fig.44 The twenty-eight *nakṣatra*-s and their width (units in Chinese degree).

This "ecliptic lodge degree" in the *Dayan li* deserves special attention. It is known as the "polar longitude" (*jihuangjing* 極黃經), and is different from the usual "ecliptic longitude" (*huangjing* 黃經).[84] *Jihuangjing* is a technical term coined by Prof. Yabuuti, who discovered that the stars in the *Shishi xingjing* 石氏星經, an ancient star catalogue of the Western Han period, were given a special kind of coordinates.[85] This coordinate system was used also in Indian astronomy. Prof. Yabuuti, who got to know the terms "polar longitude" and "polar latitude" from E. Burgess's English translation of the *Sūryasiddhānta*, translated the two terms as *jihuangjing* 極黃經 and *jihuangwei* 極黃緯 respectively. According to Prof. Neugebauer, this Indian coordinate system might have come from the work of the Greek astronomer Hipparchus. The time when this coordinate system appeared first in Chinese texts was before

Three types of coordinates

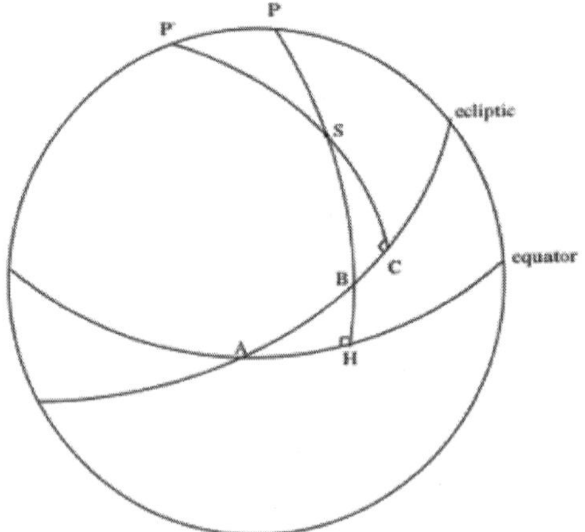

P: Equatorial pole P': Ecliptic pole A: Vernal Equinox

AH: Equatorial long. of star S **SH: Equatorial lat. of star S**

AC: Ecliptic long. of star S **SC: Ecliptic lat. of star S**

AB: Polar long. of star S **SB: Polar lat. of star S**

Fig.45 Three types of coordinates.

(© Michio Yano)

[84] See Fig.45 for the definition of polar coordinates.

[85] Yabuuti 1990:72–74.

Greek astronomy was introduced in India. While one may suggest that the Greek method was transmitted to China directly without going through India, it would be difficult to provide historical evidences for it.

It would be of interest to compute the ephemerides of the *Qiyao rangzai jue* based on this coordinate system and compare this with the positions calculated using modern astronomy. Although I have not had the time to examine those of the five planets, I have made some extremely interesting discoveries concerning the two psuedoplanets Rāhu and Ketu.

3. Rāhu and Ketu

The reason why Gautamasiddha gave the title *Jiuzhi li* 九執暦, "Astronomical table of the nine seizers," to a work that gives a summary of Indian astronomical calculation, could be that for him the "nine seizers" (*nava-graha*) represented the whole of Indian astronomy symbolically. The nine seizers or the nine luminaries (*jiuyao* 九曜) are the seven luminaries together with Rāhu and Ketu (Figs.46, 47).

Let us first examine what these two invisible planets actually refer to. In India since the ancient time, there have been two views concerning them:

1. Rāhu is the monster that causes solar and lunar eclipses. Ketu is a comet.
2. There is a monster that causes solar and lunar eclipses. Rāhu and Ketu are its head and tail respectively.

In both cases, Rāhu is related to solar and lunar eclipses. This monster appears in Indian texts since ancient times and etymologically, its name is related to the verb *rabh-*, which means "to seize." This matches the image of a Sun- or Moon-devouring monster. Ketu, however, is more problematic. The eleventh century Persian polymath al-Bīrūnī, made the following remarks in his renowned *India*:

> "The head of the dragon is called Rāhu, the tail Ketu. The Hindus seldom speak of the tail. They only use the head. In general, all comets that appear in heaven are also called Ketu."[86]

On the other hand, the Indian polymath Vahāramihira presents two chapters, entitled "Motion of Rāhu" (Ch.5) and "Motion of Ketu" (Ch.11), in his *Bṛhatsaṃhitā* for the discussion on the topic. Vahāramihira was conversant in the foreign-influenced Indian astronomy. He knew the astronomical cause for solar and lunar eclipses, writing that "the Moon enters into the Earth's shadow during lunar eclipse and enters into the Sun during solar eclipse." Thus, according to

[86] Sachau 1888:II.234.

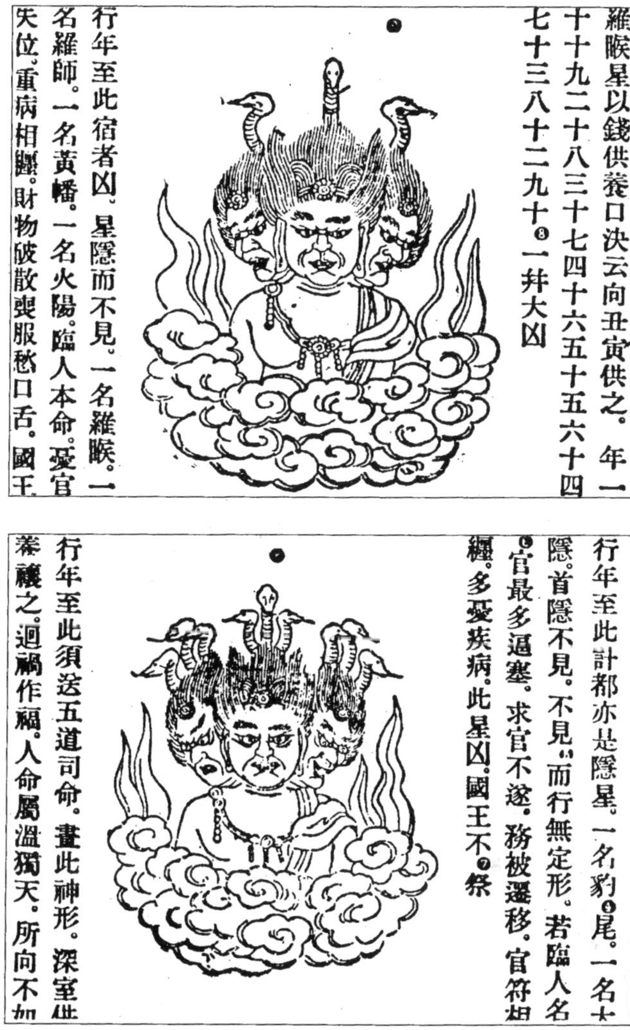

Fig.46 Rāhu (top) and Ketu (bottom) in Taishō Tripiṭaka (T 1311).

him, Rāhu is the Earth's shadow during the lunar eclipse and the Moon during the solar eclipse. On the other hand, Varāhamihira considered that Ketu were comets and there were a thousand of them.

The interpretation of Ketu as the tail part of Rāhu was also prevalent and gained popularity as time passed. If one takes a look at depictions of the *navagraha* (nine seizers) as found in modern India, one can see clearly that Rāhu and Ketu are depicted as head and tail respectively (Fig.47).

Fig.47 Rāhu (left) and Ketu (right) in India.
(© Photos courtesy of Bill M. Mak)

Fig.48 A dragon forming a coil at the ascending and descending nodes.

The myth of an eclipse-causing dragon spread throughout the entire eastern half of the Hellenistic world. The orbit of the Moon, with earth as its centre, crosses the ecliptic (path of the Sun) at an inclination of about 5°. The point where the orbit of the Moon crosses the ecliptic from south to north is called the ascending node, whereas the other crossing point at 180° opposite is called the descending node. When either the conjunction or the full moon takes place near these two nodes, a solar or lunar eclipse occurs respectively. As a result of this mythologization, the ascending and descending nodes came to be thought of as the head and the tail of a dragon which coiled up in the sky (Fig.48).

In an earlier period in India, only Rāhu was thought to be related to eclipses, although at this point there was not yet an image of a dragon. At some point, probably due to the influences from the West, the tail part of Rāhu came to be called Ketu. While the names Rāhu and Ketu are not even mentioned in the *Xiuyao jing*, by the time of the *Qiyao rangzai jue*, the two pseudoplanets are found playing an important role as members of the nine luminaries. The two luminaries also bear the following other names in the *Qiyao rangzai jue*:

> Rāhu—*Huangfan* 黄幡 ("Yellow Flag"), *Shitoushen* 蝕神頭 ("Head of the Eclipse God"), *taiyangshou* 太陽首 ("Head of the Sun").
>
> Ketu—*Baowei* 豹尾 ("Tail of Leapord"), *Shishenwei* 蝕神尾 ("Tail of the Eclipse God"), *taiyinshou* 太陰首 ("Head of the Moon).

Among these names, *Huangfan* and *Baowei* belong to the set of eight guardian gods of the Chinese Divination School of Yin-yang and are thus unrelated to India. The other two sets of names, however, are clearly of Western origin.

The ascending and descending nodes are not fixed on the ecliptic but revolves around the ecliptic in retrograde motion once every 18.5 years. To calculate solar and lunar eclipses, one must compute the positions of the nodes, taking into consideration the period of this retrograde motion. Thus, Indian astronomical works treat the nodes (in particular, the ascending node) as if they were astral bodies and try to work out their astronomical values. In this way, Rāhu and Ketu are elevated to the status of *graha*, in line with the other seven luminaries, to create the group of what is called the nine luminaries or the nine seizers.

4. Interpretation of Ketu and Its Astronomical Implications

Now that we understand the reason why there is a table for Rāhu in the *Qiyao rangzai jue*, let us first examine the mean motion of Rāhu, which is given as follows:

19^{d}	$1^{\circ\circ}$
1^{m}	$1\frac{6}{10}^{\circ\circ}$
1^{y}	$19\frac{1}{3}^{\circ\circ}$
1.5^{y}	one *ci* 次 (one-twelfth of one Rotation)
18^{y}	one Rotation—$11\frac{2}{3}^{\circ\circ}$
93^{y}	one Big Cycle (*daizhong* 大終)

The value $365\frac{1}{4}^{\circ\circ}$ less $11\frac{2}{3}^{\circ\circ}$ in eighteen years, if converted to modern units, is about 348.5°. In other words, there would be about five rotations in ninety-three years and one rotation takes about 18.6 years. As a result, the ephemeris of Rāhu in the *Qiyao rangzai jue* spans ninety-three years. As for the Epoch of this particular ephemeris, unlike those of the five planets (794 CE), the first year of *Yuanhe* 元和 (806 CE) was chosen instead.

To compare the ephemeris in the *Qiyao rangzai jue* with modern astronomical values, I calculated the position of the ascending node on 15 February 806 CE, using Brown's formula, with the assumption that the Epoch was on the date for solar-term *Yushui* 雨水. Converting the "$10^{\circ\circ}$ of *Zhen* 軫" into modern longitude, the resulting values of the ascending node are:

According to Brown's formula: 175.74°

According to *Qiyao rangzai jue*: $177.6^{\circ\circ}$ (= 175.04° translator's note)

Thus, Rāhu is clearly the Moon's ascending node.

If Ketu were the descending node, one would not need to prepare a separate ephemeris for Ketu, as it would be in fact exactly 180° from Rāhu. Despite that logic, there is a table for Ketu in the *Qiyao rangzai jue*, preceded by the following values for its mean motion:

9^{d}	$1^{\circ\circ}$
1^{m}	$3\frac{4}{10}{}^{\circ\circ}$
9^{m}	one *ci* 次 (one-twelfth of one Rotation)
1^{y}	$40\frac{7}{10}{}^{\circ\circ}$
9^{y}	one Rotation minus $6\frac{3}{10}{}^{\circ\circ}$
62^{y}	seven Rotations minus $3\frac{4}{10}{}^{\circ\circ}$

It was pointed out by Prof. Yabuuti that since these values roughly agree with the motion of the lunar perigee, Ketu in the *Qiyao rangzai jue* might have been considered the perigee—something quite new in the history of ancient astronomy. As I thought this was a particularly interesting hypothesis, I tried comparing the position of Ketu at the Epoch with that of the lunar perigee as calculated by modern astronomical method. The result was quite surprising. The position of Ketu:

According to Brown's formula: 104.67°
According to *Qiyao rangzai jue*: 291.7°° (286.8° translator's note)

Since such a conspicuous error is hardly imaginable, I came to realize that if one adds 180° to the result based on Brown's formula, one arrives at a value (284.67°) quite close to that of the *Qiyao rangzai jue*. In other words, there is a possibility that the Ketu described in the *Qiyao rangzai jue* refers to the lunar apogee.

As the lunar motion is irregular, it was studied in detail in Greek astronomy as well. In Ptolemy's system, geometrical models for the explanation of lunar motion and data from its mean motion table are used as a basis for planetary theory. The lunar apogee is important as the starting point for such calculations and its periodicity had been studied in detail. In Indian astronomy, which was influenced by Greek astronomy, the apogee was called *ucca* and became an object of study. In particular, since the motion of the lunar apogee is rapid, it was treated as an imaginary astral body just like the ascending node. Generally in the history of ancient astronomy in both Greece and India, the apogee has been considered important while the perigee has been ignored. Therefore, it is not strange to consider that the lunar apogee would come to be called "Ketu" and was regarded as one of the nine luminaries. Since such a strange interpretation is not found in any Indian text, this can perhaps be a unique and arbitrary interpretation of the *Qiyao rangzai jue*.

Surprising as it is, this unique interpretation of Ketu was adopted among the Japanese astrologers of Sukuyōdō. That becomes clear in my examination of the two Japanese horoscopes in the next section.

5. Japanese Horoscopes

About two hundred years after Kūkai brought the *Xiuyao jing* to Japan, the astrological school of Sukuyōdō became popular in Japan. During the two hundred years, other texts such as the *Duliyusi jing* and the *Qiyao rangzai jue* had no doubt exerted their influences. However, it was the *Futian li* 符天曆 (Jp. *Futenreki*) that played the most important role.

For 823 years, from 862 to 1684 CE, the *Xuanming li* 宣明曆 (Jp. *Senmyōreki*) was used as the official calendar in Japan. However, among the Sukuyōdō astrologers, the *Futian li* was used instead. This shows their antagonism toward the Onmyōdō astrologers as shown by Momo Hiroyuki's 1969 study. While the *Futian li* is mentioned as a title in Chinese historical records, the work itself has long been lost.

Recently, however, a solar motion table titled "Table of Solar Motion according to the *Futian li*" (*Futian li jingrichancha licheng* 符天曆經日纏差立成) was discovered in the Tenri University Library. Part of this mysterious astronomical work has thus come into light. The documents known as *Sukuyōkanmon* 宿曜勘文 attributed to Sukuyōdō astrologers have been collected by Momo, who showed that the works were directly related to the *Futian li* in a number of instances. According to Momo, these documents contributed greatly toward the development of the astrological school of Sukuyōdō.

The *Futian li* was compiled by Cao Shiwei 曹士蒍 toward the end of the eighth century during the Tang Period. From a record titled "Sitiankao" 司天考 of the *New Historical Records of the Five Dynasties* (*Xinwudaishi* 新五代史), we know that the *Futian li* set the Epoch at the solar term *Yushui* 雨水 in 660 CE. Yabuuti, on the other hand, found an explanatory remark in the one-fascicled "Luoji eryinyao lichengli" 羅計二隱曜立成曆 of the twelfth fascicle of *Zhizhai shulu jieti* 直齋書錄解題 by Chen Zhensun 陳振孫 of the Southern Sung Period:

稱大中大夫曹士蔿。亦莫知何人。但云起元和元年入曆。

There was a *Dazhong dafu* 大中大夫 named Cao Shiwei. No one knows who he was. But it was said that he prepared the ephemerides based on the Epoch of first year of Yuanhe (806 CE)

In other words, the Epoch of 806 CE was used for the ephemerides of Rāhu and Ketu. As discussed earlier, the ephemerides of Rāhu and Ketu in the *Qiyao rangzai jue* also used 806 CE as the Epoch (the Epoch of 794 CE was used for the ephemerides of the five planets). The author of the *Qiyao rangzai jue* was clearly aware of the *Futian li* when he made the remark that the year 806 CE was 147 years after the Epoch, that is, that of the *Futian li* (660 CE).

As far as the ephemerides of Rāhu and Ketu are concerned, the *Futian li* and the *Qiyao rangzai jue* resemble each other to a large extent. In 957 CE the Tendai monk *Nichien* 日延 brought to Japan the *Futian li*, which included the ephemerides (Ch. *licheng,* Jp. *rissei* 立成). Subsequently, Buddhist astrology evolved using texts such as *Futian li*, without relying on the divinatory school of Onmyōdō or the traditional calendrical school.

The texts which the diviners of the Onmyōdō School used to explain their divination are called "Divination Reports" 勘文 (Jp. *kamon* or *kanmon*). Momo Hiroyuki collected *kanmon* documents written by the Sukuyōdō astrologers—a total of sixteen "Sukuyō Divination Reports" or *sukuyōkamon*. These he divided into four categories:

Type I: "Divination Report for Birth Year" 生年勘文—two extant examples

Type II: "Divination Report for Particular Year" 行年勘文—seven extant examples

Type III: "Divination Report for Solar Eclipses" 日食勘文—three extant examples

Type IV: "Divination Report for Lunar Eclipses" 月食勘文—four extant examples

According to Momo, the first type is divination based on the position of stars according to the person's time of birth; in other words, genethliacal astrology. The second type is "divination of a person's fortune in a particular year based on the planetary movement of that year." The remaining two types are divinations based on solar and lunar eclipses. The most interesting among these are the works on natal astrology, of which two horoscope have survived with complete diagrams that show the positions of the nine luminaries. A comparison is made between the content of these works and modern astronomical data in the next section.

Horoscope of the Third Year of Ten'ei 天永三年 (1113 CE)

Astrological record *Sukuyō unmei kanroku* 宿曜運命勘録.[87]

1. Date

天永三年〈壬辰〉十二月二十五日〈戊申〉時丑誕生男
大寒初日

Male, born third year of Ten'ei (*renchen* [29]), twenty-fifth day (*wushen* [45]) of the twelfth month, hour of *chou* 丑. First day of the solar-term "Major Cold" (*dahan* 大寒).

Note: In modern terms, this is 15 January, 1113 CE, Wednesday, around 2:00 a.m. (hour of *chou*). In ancient Japan the calendar date changes at 4:00 a.m. (hour of *yin* 寅).

2. Calculation

算勘
自上元庚申歲距今日所積日數。十六萬五千四百二十八日。
紀法八　當己酉
政法四　水曜直

Calculation
Number of accumulated days from the Epoch in the year of *Gengshen* [57] to today: 165,428 days.
Remainder from the sexagenary calculation: Eight, which is *jiyou* 己酉 [46].
Remainder from the seven-day calculation: Four, which falls on Wednesday.

Note: The accumulated number of days is calculated from the Epoch, which is set to the first day of the first month of the fifth year of *Xianqing* 顯慶五年 (660 CE). Dividing this number (165428) by sixty (*jifa* 紀法), one obtains the remainder eight. Since the sexagenary year of the Epoch is *renyin* 壬寅, the remainder eight corresponds to the sexagenary year *jiyou* 己酉. If one divides the

[87] *Zoku gunsho ruijū* 続群書類従, p.908.

accumulated number of days (165428) by seven (*zhengfa* 政法), one obtains four as the remainder. Since the Epoch was on a Sunday, this date would be a Wednesday. However, this sexagenary year and the weekday agrees with the reality only if we assume that the day starts from midnight.[88]

3. Position of the Nine Luminaries in degrees

九曜行度

太陽盈曆行女宿五度十九分。
太陰遲曆行尾宿四度九十三分。
歲星後退行井宿廿一度三十分。
熒惑前順遲行翌宿初九十三分。
鎮星後順行室宿九度三十二分。
太白後伏行女宿九度九十五分。
辰星前順續行危宿四度十分。
蝕神頭運行奎宿一度十四分。
蝕神尾順行軫宿九度四十四分。

Position of the Nine Luminaries in degrees:
Sun, ahead of mean position, 5.19°° of *Nü* 女.
Moon, behind mean position, 4.93°° of *Wei* 尾.
Jupiter, in second retrogradation (Θ to Ψ),[89] 21.30°° of *Jing* 井.
Mars, in first progression (Γ to Φ), slow motion, 0.93°° of *Yi* 翼 (emend.).
Saturn, in second progression (Ψ to Ω), 9.32°° of *Shi* 室.
Venus, in second invisibility (Ω to Γ), 9.95°° of *Nü* 女.
Mercury, in first progression (> Ξ), 4.10°° of *Wei* 危.
Eclipse God Head (Rāhu), in motion (sic.), 1.14°° of *Kui* 奎.
Eclipse God Tail (Ketu), in progression, 9.44°° of *Zhen* 軫.

Note: This shows the positions of the Sun, the Moon, the five planets, Rāhu and Ketu at the time of the native's birth. These are indicated using the coordinates of the twenty-eight lodges. Therefore, their actual positions cannot be established unless those coordinates are known. For the time being, taking the approximate values of the ecliptic

[88] Yabuuti 1976:10.

[89] For planetary phenomena, see Neugebauer 1969:126–27.

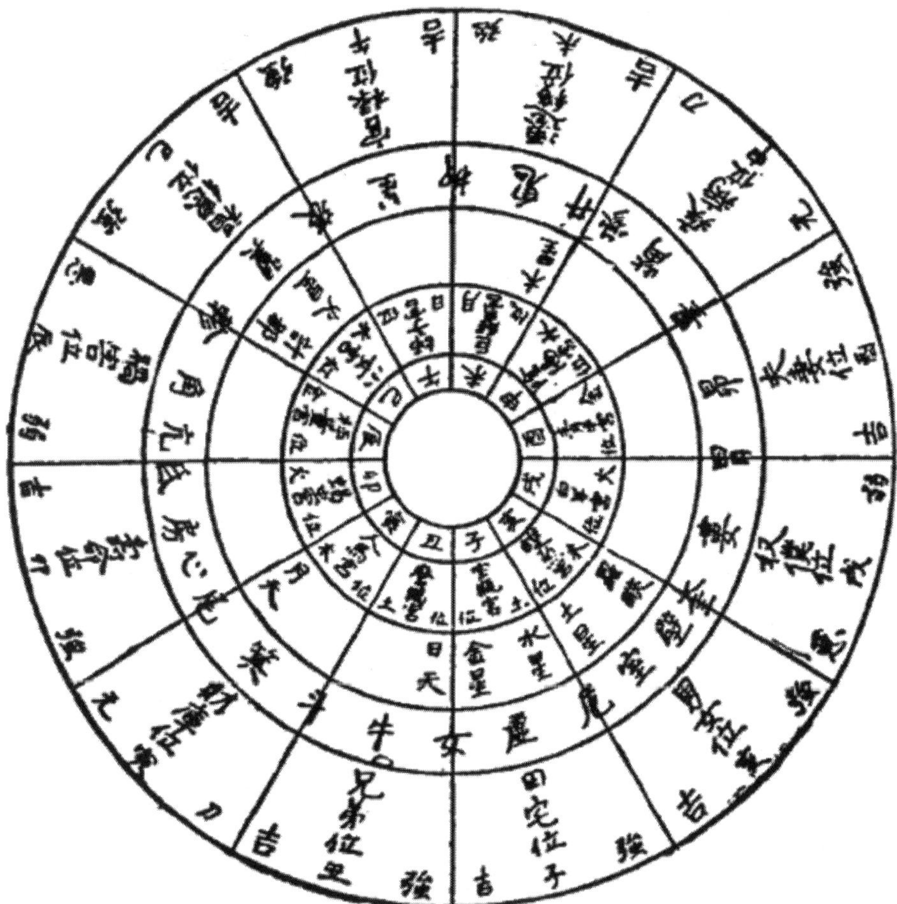

Fig.49 Horoscope of the third year of Teiei 天永三年 (1113 CE).

longitude of the nine luminaries based on the coordinates of the *Qiyao rangzai jue* as shown in Fig.44, I calculated the ecliptic longitude of the standard stars in 1100 CE. Then I compared these with the values of the Sun, Moon and five planets based on Tuckerman's computer-generated table. As for Rāhu which was known as the "Eclipse God Head," I calculated the position of the ascending node based on Brown's formula. A summary of the values may be found in Fig.50.

Ketu, known also as the "Eclipse God Tail," remains a problem. In both my calculation as well as the horoscope of Fig.49, the position

	Kamon values	I. Ecliptic longitude	II. From Tuckerman's Table
Sun	*Nü* 女 5.19°°	302.64°	301.3°
Moon	*Wei* 尾 4.93°°	245.08°	240.3°
Jupiter	*Jing* 井 21.30°°	103.79°	107.0°
Mars	*Yi* 翼 0.93°°	153.96°	167.4°
Saturn	*Shi* 室 9.32°°	342.28°	347.7°
Venus	*Nü* 女 9.95°°	307.33°	292.3°
Mercury	*Wei* 危 4.10°°	321.38°	319.5°
Rāhu	*Kui* 奎 1.14°°	0.97°	359.3° (Ascending node)*
Ketu	*Zhen* 軫 9.44°°	181.16°	173.5° (Lunar apogee)*

Fig.50 Analysis of Horoscope of 3rd year of Ten'ei 天永三年 (1113 CE).

Note: Chinese degree °°, modern degree ° (*based on Brown's Formula)

of Ketu is found to be at around 180° away from Rāhu. Therefore, everyone would have thought that Ketu, being literally the "Tail" was the descending node of the Moon. In fact, no one has ever doubted that. However, in the text it was written that the "Eclipse God Tail" moves in *progressive* motion. If it were the descending node of the Moon, it should have been in *retrograde* motion instead. It may be noted that the text which describes the "Eclipse God Head in motion" 蝕神頭運行, where the word "in motion" *yunxing* 運行 is definitely a mistake and should be emended as *nixing* 逆行 (in retrograde motion).

In the annual "Divination Report" which follows—which describes the fate of the querist from his fortieth to fifty-seventh years—I found that Ketu moved in the direction of increasing ecliptic longitude. Thus this cannot be the descending node in any way. When I tried to obtain the longitude of the lunar apogee using Brown's Formula, I found that the value is not far from the position of Ketu.

As I will show in the following pages using yet another horoscope, the possibility of Ketu being the lunar apogee (as in the *Qiyao rangzai jue*) turns out to be not a mere conjecture, but a matter of certainty.

Horoscope of the Fifth Year of Bun'ei 文永五年 (1268 CE)

Astrological Records *Sukuyō on-unroku* 宿曜御運錄[90]

1. Date

文永六［五］年〈戊辰〉六月〈己未〉廿六日〈丙午〉時亥御誕生男

当立秋七日

Male, born sixth (emended to fifth) year of Ten'ei (*wuchen* [5]), twenty-sixth day (*bingwu* [43]) of the sixth month, hour of *hai* 亥. Seventh day of the solar-term "Start of Autumn" (*liqiu* 立秋).

Note: In modern terms, 6 August, 1268 CE, around 10:00 p.m.

2. Calculation

竿勘

積日廿万二千二百卌五日

紀法五丙午

政法二月曜

Calculation
Number of accumulated days: 222,245 days.
Remainder from the sexagenary calculation: Five, which is *bingwu* 丙午 [43].
Remainder from the seven-day calculation: Two, which falls on Monday.

Note: If one divides the sum of days (222245) from the Epoch by sixty, one obtains five as the remainder. If one divides it (222245) by seven, one obtains two as the remainder. As a result, the sexagenary day of the date is *bingwu* 丙午 and the weekday is Monday.

[90] From the collection of Rokujō Kōichi 六条弘一.

3. Position of the Nine Luminaries in degrees

九曜行度
日天子縮曆行張宿三度。
月天子疾曆行井宿六度。
木星前伏行張宿十度。
火星前次疾行畢宿十三度。
土星前順行井宿廿三度。
金星前順行軫宿一度。
水星後逆行星宿六度。
羅睺星逆行房宿一度。
計都星順行婁宿十度。

Position of the Nine Luminaries in degrees
Sun the Hevenly Son, behind mean position, $3^{\circ\circ}$ of *Zhang* 張.
Moon the Hevenly Son, ahead of mean position, $6^{\circ\circ}$ of *Jing* 井.
Jupiter, in first invisibility (> Ω), $10^{\circ\circ}$ of *Zhang* 張.
Mars, in second progression (?) (Ψ to Ω), fast motion, $13^{\circ\circ}$ of *Bi* 畢.
Saturn, in first progression (Γ to Φ), $23^{\circ\circ}$ of *Jing* 井.
Venus, in first progression (> Γ), $1^{\circ\circ}$ of *Zhen* 軫.
Mercury, in second retrogradation (< Ω), $6^{\circ\circ}$ of *Xing* 星.
Eclipse God Head (Rāhu), in retrogradation, $1^{\circ\circ}$ of *Fang* 房.
Eclipse God Tail (Ketu), in progression, $10^{\circ\circ}$ of *Lou* 婁.

Note: With the same method as described previously, let us try to compare the ecliptic longitudes from the text and the ones according to modern astronomy (Fig.52). By just looking at the horoscope, it is clear that Rāhu and Ketu are not positioned diametrically opposite to each other. The actual positions are in fact separated by over 200°. Nonetheless, Ketu's position is not far off from the actual position of the lunar apogee.

Here, it becomes clear that Ketu in the Japanese astrological school of Sukuyōdō, despite also being called the "Eclipse God Tail," was actually the lunar apogee. However, such a peculiar interpretation was noted also in the *Qiyao rangzai jue* as we have already seen. Regardless of what the ephemerides (Ch. *richeng* 立成) of Rāhu and Ketu might have actually looked like in the *Futian li* which is no longer existent, it is now clear that Rāhu and Ketu are the ascending lunar node and the lunar apogee respectively. The constants for their motion would have been practically the same as those in the *Qiyao rangzai jue*.

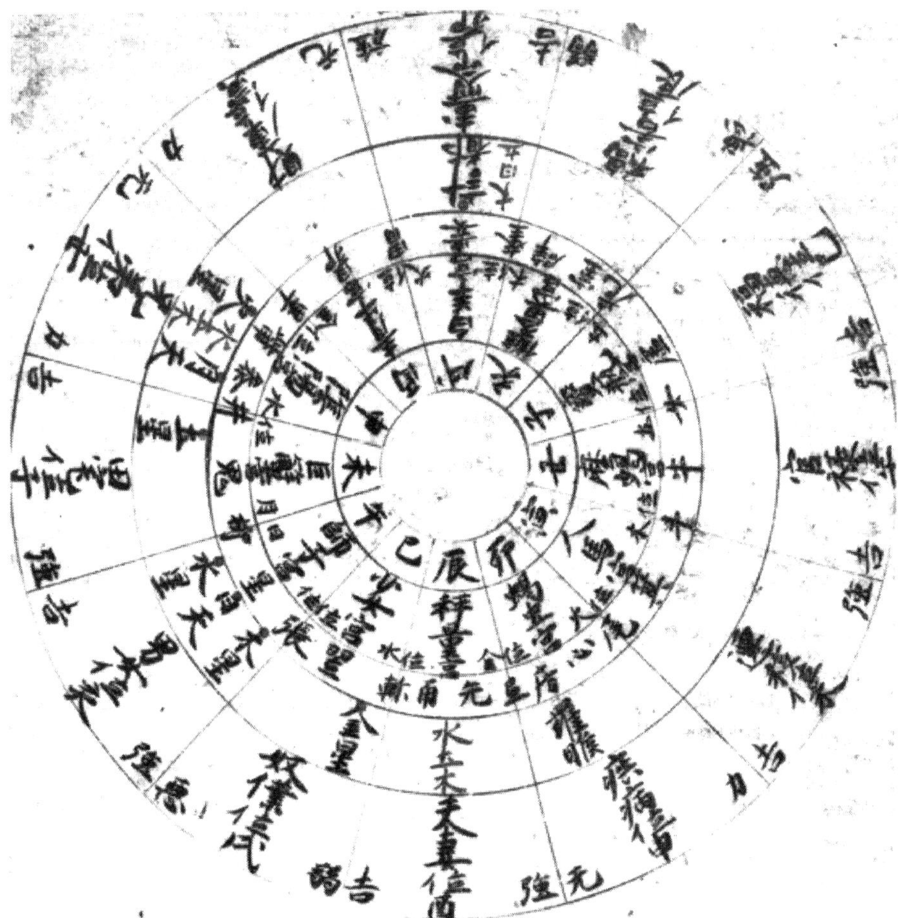

Fig.51 Horoscope of 5th year of Bun'ei 文永五年 (1268 CE) (Nakayama 1969:61).

	Kamon values	I. Ecliptic longitude	II. From Tuckerman's Table
Sun	*Zhang* 張 3°°	139.5°	141.2°
Moon	*Jing* 井 6°°	91°	98.5°
Jupiter	*Zhang* 張 10°°	146.5°	150.0°
Mars	*Bi* 畢 13°°	71.8°	84.2°
Saturn	*Jing* 井 23°°	107.8°	109.1°
Venus	*Zhen* 軫 1°°	175.2°	177.3°
Mercury	*Xing* 星 6°°	136.4°	129.3°
Rghu	*Fang* 房 1°°	232.3°	230.7° (Ascending node of Moon)*
Ketu	*Lou* 婁 10°°	30.3°	23.36° (Lunar apogee)*

Fig.52 Analysis of Horoscope of 5th year of Bun'ei 文永五年 (1268 CE).

Note: Chinese degree °°, modern degree ° (*based on Brown's Formula)

Sukuyōdō Astrologers Who Used the *Qiyao rangzai jue*

The two books *Qiyao rangzai jue* and *Futian li*, which were probably of Central Asian origin, found a common home in the Japanese astrological school of Sukuyōdō. The ephemerides given in the *Qiyao rangzai jue* are not particularly accurate, as planetary positions are given only in monthly intervals. As a result it may have been impossible to give the planetary positions with the degree of precision required to make a horoscope for a particular day. Nonetheless, if used skillfully, the *Qiyao rangzai jue* was probably useful enough for slow moving planets such as Saturn and Jupiter. For people who did not possess advanced texts such as *Futian li*, this could well be the case. In fact as it will be shown, one can be certain about the existence of some Sukuyōdō astrologers who made use of the ephemeris of the *Qiyao rangzai jue*.

As has been previously mentioned (p.130), these ephemerides were tabulated one year per column with the year of each planet's synodic period written at the top of each column. It has been noted already that the Epoch for the five planets was set at 794 CE, while the one for Rāhu and Ketu was set at 806 CE (p.140). However, in both the Taishō edition as well as the manuscript Momo made available to me, in the head margin right above the year, one or two sexagenary years are written. Japanese era names are sometimes also given. For example, in the table for Jupiter cited earlier, the first three years are given as follows (Fig.43 and Fig.53):

寛徳元		
乙酉 戊申	甲申 丁未	癸未 丙午
三	二	一年

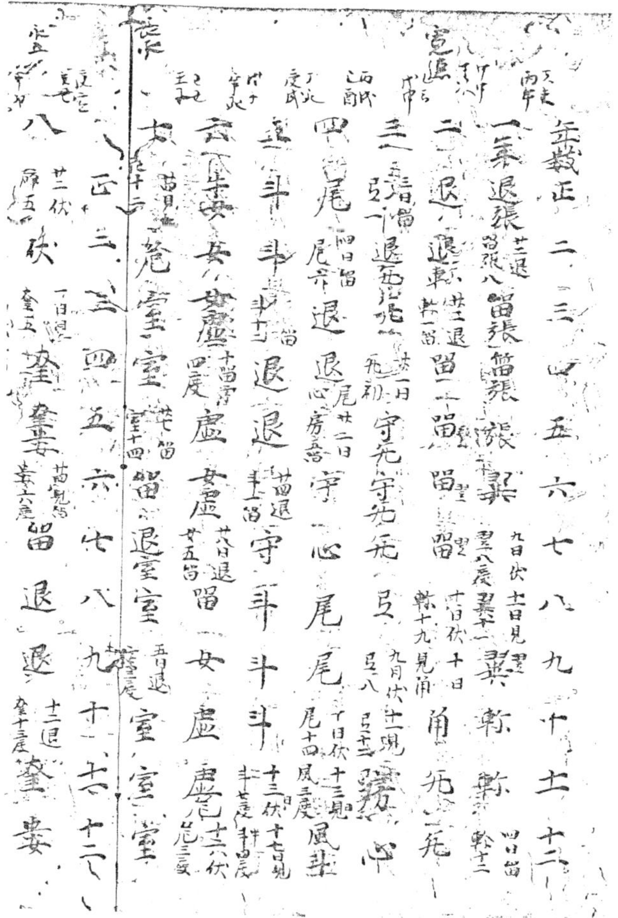

Fig.53 Planetary ephemeris in *Qiyao rangzai jue* (beginning of Jupiter).

The synodic period for Jupiter was set to be eighty-three years. If one supposes the cycle repeats itself correctly, the Japanese era name, the sexagenary year and the Western date of the first year for each cycle would be (from the first up to the sixth) as follows:

1st cycle	13th year of Enryaku 延曆十三年	*Jiaxu* 甲戌	794
2nd cycle	1st year of Gangyō 元慶元年	*Dingyou* 丁酉	877
3rd cycle	4th year of Tentoku 天德四年	*Gengshen* 庚申	960
4th cycle	4th year of Chōkyū 長久四年	*Guiwei* 癸未	1043
5th cycle	1st year of Taiji 大治元年	*Bingwu* 丙午	1126
6th cycle	3rd year of Shōgen 承元三年	*Jisi* 己巳	1209

Of the two sexagenary years written above the first year, *Guiwei* 癸未 is first year of the fourth cycle, which is the fourth year of Chōkyū (1043). In fact, the following year is the first year of Kantoku 寬德元年, with the sexagenary year of *Jiashen* 甲申 (1044), just as it was written on the table. As for *Bingwu* 丙午, *Dingwei* 丁未, *Xushen* 戌申 which are written on the left, they show the years of fifth cycle starting from the first year of Taiji (1126).

After checking all the head margin dates, it became clear to me that these sexagenary years and Japanese era names span roughly from the tenth to the thirteenth century. In other words, the Japanese Sukuyōdō astrologers who had copies of this table had actually made use of this table during this period.

As for the Japanese era names inserted into the manuscript, they appear to be irregular and few. More frequent are the markings with the characters *gannen* 元年 which indicate the change of era.[91] What is interesting is that in all the ephemerides, the second year of Gen'ei 元永二年 (1119) is indicated in the margin. I suspect that this was the birth year of someone whose horoscope the astrologer (probably Chinya 珎也 who received the manuscript in 1116 CE as mentioned in p.120) was asked to prepare.

We do not know whether the astrologer made the correct horoscope for his client. At any rate, it is clear that the *Qiyao rangzai jue* has a mathematical side, which one would not guess from merely its title. This work can in fact be said to have an exceptional place among esoteric Buddhist astrological works.

91 Yano 1995:81.

Horoscope Reading

The horoscope of the third year of Ten'ei (sexagenary year *renchen* 壬辰) we have just seen is one for a man who was born in that year. In the *Zoku gunsho ruijū* one also finds various comments attached to the diagram. Here let us take a look at its content.

> The original birth year 本命辰 is the God *Renchen* 壬辰—The sexagenary year of the birth year of this man is *Renchen*.
>
> The original birth mansion 本命宿 is *Wei* 尾—At the birth of this man, the Moon was at *Mūla* (or the lodge *Wei*).
>
> The original birth sign 本命宮 in Scorpio—At the time of birth, the Ascendent sign was Scorpio.
>
> The original governing sign 本主宮 is Sagittarius—At the time of birth, the Moon was in Sagittarius.

As for the term *sanfangzhu* 三方主 in the following sentence, the meaning is unknown. After the general explanation of the auspiciousness and inauspiciousness of the mansions and the luminaries over the person's life, the prediction of this person's fortune is given under five headings:[92]

> Chapter on Hereditary Nature 天性章
> Chapter on Good Fortune [with reference to other Buddhist Sūtras] 榮福章
> Chapter on Fate 運命章
> Chapter on Miscellaneous Fortune [on Human Relations] 諸運章
> Chapter on [Fortune of] Particular Years 行年章

Various texts are quoted by the author with explanations on the prediction. While in some cases passages are simply cited as coming from a certain "sūtra," the cited texts with titles include the *Wenshu jing* 文殊經 (*Mañjuśrī Sūtra*?), *Yusi jing* 聿斯經 (*Tetrabiblos*?), *Wuxing ding fen* 五行定分, *Xiuyao jing* 宿曜經, *Daji jing* 大集經 *Mahāsaṃnipāta-sūtra*, *Rizang jing* 日藏經 (*Sūryagarbhasūtra*) and [*Qiyao*]*rangzai*[jue] [七曜]攘災[决]. Among these, the quotes from the *Yusi jing*, which was discussed earlier, are of particular interest. Here are some of the technical terms ascribed to the *Yusi jing* in this astrological work:

---

[92] Yano 1988:109.

Saturn in the Sign of Jupiter 土在木宮—Saturn in Pisces, governed by Jupiter.

Jupiter in the Sign of the Moon 木在月宮—Jupiter in Cancer, governed by the Moon.

Saturn in trine to Jupiter 土木三合—Saturn about 120° from Jupiter.

Mars in trine to the Sun 火日三合—Mars about 120° from the Sun.

Venus and Mercury in the same Sign 金水同宮—Venus and Mercury together in Aquarius.

All these technical terms are in fact used in Western astrology. Even if the *Yusi jing* turns out not to be Ptolemy's *Tetrabiblos*, it is without any doubt that it is a work that belongs to the tradition of Western astrology.

Chapter Five—Additional Notes

About Chinya

Information about the astrologer known as Chinya, the owner of the *Qiyao rangzai jue* (photos of whose manuscripts I obtained from Momo Hiroyuki), can be found in Murayama Shūichi, *Nihon onmyōdōshi sōsetsu* 日本陰陽道総説, 1981. Based on the *Chōshūki* 長秋記 of Minamoto no Morotoki (1077–1136 CE), the text describes, the debate between the Sukuyōdō astrologer Gensan 源算 and specialists in Chinese calendars over whether the seventh month of the fourth year of Taiji (大治, 1129 CE) was a big (30 days) or small (29 days) month. The Sukuyōdō astrologer Chinya is described as a supporter of Gensan (p.226). Murayama notes that Chinya was succeeded by his disciples Chinka 珍賀, Chinzen 珍善, and Chinyō 珍誉.

VI. INDIAN ASTROLOGY TODAY

We have seen how Western astrology, a product out of the melting pot of Hellenism in which elements from Babylonia, Egypt and Greece melded together, arrived in India. It merged with the indigenous divination of India and formed a new kind of astrology that eventually arrived in Japan through China. Although it flourished in Japan toward the end of the Heian Period, it did not in fact survive for very long. Prof. Momo explained that the practice of Sukuyōdō in its pure form lasted until the Nanbokuchō period or, at most, around the beginning of the Muromachi Period. Nonetheless, in the form of expiatory rites, it continued to be practiced in Esoteric Buddhism and was passed down to scholarly monks like Morita Ryūsen into the twentieth century. In a way, it is still alive, and books attempting to revive the practice may be found today.

Western astrology has even become a fad among some young people today here in Japan. Astrology columns, in which prediction according to the zodiacal signs are given, are found in the weekly magazines. How many people would ever realize that the astrology known as Sukuyōdō, having the same origin as the Western one, was once popular in Japan as far back as a thousand years ago? Thanks to the advance of science, young people can find out the planetary positions from astronomical almanacs based on computer calculation without having to rely anymore on the *Qiyao rangzai jue* or the *Futian li*.

Additional Notes of Chapter 6

(1) My subsequent and more recent visits to India

In the rest of Chapter 6 of the first edition I included a report of my visit to India in 1985. Since it has some meaning as a report from more than thirty years ago I kept it in the second edition, but in this English translation it is not included. Since 1985 I had many chances to visit India and I collected a large number of traditional Indian almanacs (*pañcāṅga*). I visited astrologers and *pañcāṅga* makers and kept interview records. In the following I would like to write about some of my visits to India.

In 1991 I visited India three times including Nepal once. Records of my visits may partly be found in my book *Senseijutsushi-tachi-no Indo*, "The Astrologers' India" (Tokyo, 1992). At that time I brought a laptop computer which contained the first version of my Indian calendar program, as I wanted to ask the professionals for their opinions on the program.

In December 1992 I visited Prof. Warier at a small village located about 100 miles north from Trivandrum. I was much impressed by him who was teaching modern astronomy while trying at the same time to keep the framework of traditional learning. I contributed a report of this visit to the Japanese journal *Yuriika*, "Eureka" (June, 1993).

After several years, I visited Kerala for three years consecutively. In 2010 at an international conference in Kozhikode (old Calicut) in which I participated, I met an astrologer who used seashells for his computation. I wrote about him in my book *Mathematical Way of Thinking in India*. In 2011, I had an opportunity to see the *Agnicayana* ceremony which took place in a village near Trissur in central Kerala. I video-recorded my interview with the astrologers who used seashells and pebbles for calculation. In 2012, I visited the Manuscript Library in Trivandrum and took photos of many manuscripts of astronomical texts. There I met Prof. K.V. Sarma's son, who told me that he was just beginning to learn the computation with seashells. In Kerala, along with the luni-solar calendar, the solar calendar based on the traditional *nirayana* (sidereal) method was also used, in which the beginning of the year is *Siṃhasaṃkrānti* (Sun's entry in Leo) which falls on around 17 August in the modern calendar.

(2) Visit to Nepal

In Chapter Four of the *Senseijutsushi-tachi-no Indo* I wrote about my visit to Nepal. After nearly twenty years I made another visit to Kathumandu in 2011. Prof. Nayaraj Pant whom I met in 1991 had passed away, but I could meet his son Prof. Mahesh Pant in his home. He showed me the very precious manuscript collection of his father. Prof. Pant was keen to publish a note on his father's collection and to preserve it for the future generation.

I heard a rumor that Mr. Joshi, whom I met in 1991 as the Royal Astrologer, might have been implicated in the massacre of the Royal family in 2001. When I met him he boasted that he prepared all the horoscopes of the Royal Family. According to an e-newspaper from Nepal, Mr. Joshi, who was questioned by mass media, replied that the horoscopes were lost. Since he died soon after the truth remains unknown.

In Nepal there was the so-called 'Maoist Revolution' in 2008 and the monarchy was abolished. There is no more the official post of Royal Astrologer, but the traditional almanac and astrology still play important roles in the daily life. The Director of the Calendar Committee in the Science Academy of the Government succeeded the works of the Royal Astrologer. The Committee oversees matters related to the traditional almanacs. In 2011, I met the Director of the Committee, Dr. Dungel. According to him all the traditional almanacs published in Nepal should be authorized by him. He himself is the author of an almanac called *Sūryapañcāṅga*, whose name suggested that the calendar was related to the *Sūryasiddhānta*. Since my program is based on the *Sūryasiddhānta*, it is natural that the values in the Nepalese almanacs overseen by Dr. Dungel are very close to those produced by my program. According to him, since lunar and solar eclipses should be predicted correctly, the eclipse computations were made according to modern astronomy. A computer software for the traditional almanac was developed and was on sale, but it is so expensive that it was used only by professional astrologers and publishers.

Out of the nine almanacs which I received from this Committee, eight turned out to have the same dates corresponding to the modern calendar, although their cover pages appeared different. The beginning of the year was 14 April of the modern calendar which was the day when the Sun entered the Indian Aries (*Meṣa*). At first glance this is similar to the south Indian solar calendar, but after several days from the beginning of the year, the calendar becomes a type of *pūrṇimānta* ("ending with full moon") system. Only one almanac among all starts the year on the first day of the white half of Kārttika month and on the next page is shown the dark half of Mārgaśīrṣa month; it is thus based on the *pūrṇimānta* system. According to Mr. Dungel, this particular one was written in the Newar language and was used by the 'Maoists'.

(3) Pañcāṅga

Fig.54 of the first edition is a photo of 'a boy selling *pañcāṅgas*' and Fig.55 is captioned 'an example of modern *pañcāṅga*.' Actually they are of the wall-hung type and the main framework is that of the western calendar, with only additional notes on traditional elements around the western date. Strictly speaking, we cannot call them *pañcāṅga*. The real *pañcāṅga* is of oblong shape with a longer horizontal side. Each page is allotted to a half-month. All the five elements: *tithi*, weekday, *nakṣatra*, *yoga*, and *karaṇa*, are shown. Also the time of sunrise, moonrise, and traditional solar elements are given. Sometimes it is not easy to find the corresponding western date. There is a great variety of *pañcāṅgas* and many are based on modern astronomy, but still some are based on Sanskrit astronomical texts. The most frequently used text is the *Sūryasiddhānta*. Such kind of almanac corresponds closely to the *pañcāṅga* program which I wrote with the help of Dr. Makoto Fushimi.

In the *Senseijutush-itachi-no Indo*, I wrote about the variety of Indian almanacs. In 2010 I witnessed a heated discussion among the *Pañcāṅga* makers at a conference which was held in Tirumala in the State of Andhra Pradesh. This conference, called Hindu Dharma Acharya Sabha, was convened by the top authorities of Hinduism. I learned how the almanac was strongly connected to the rituals. The most important topic of discussion was whether the traditional almanac should be based on the *nirayaṇa* (sidereal) method or the *sāyana* (with precession) method. Another point of discussion was to what extent they would utilize modern astronomy. One of the participants of this conference was a computer programming expert, who placed his program (in Tamil language) on his website.

As I wrote in the *Senseijutushi-tachi-no Indo*, the use of computer in astrology was gradually becoming popular. An increasing number of people are switching their calculation from the traditional manual way to the computer-generated way.

After my presentation in the conference in Tirumala I got a message from one of the participants. He was Prof. Ramchandra Pandey, the person whom I had met in Benares Hindu University in 1991. I wrote about him in the *Senseijutush-itachi-no Indo*. I was very glad to know that he remembered me. I accepted his invitation and visited the Jyotiṣa department of BHU on the return trip from Kathmandu in the summer of 2011. I met the professors and graduate students in the Department of Jyotiṣa and Pañcāṅga and got some important information. The Chair Professor of the Pañcāṅga Section, who is the successor of Prof. Pandey, is responsible for the annual publication of the Pañcāṅga of the University. What was most interesting to me was that in this Department the computer was not used at all and all the calculations were made manually. At that time of the year they were very busy preparing the calendar of the following year.

Postscript

As a Japanese who conducts research on Indian astronomy and astrology, I have always thought that it is incumbent on me to clarify the origin of the *Xiuyao jing*. Therefore, when I was asked by Professor Nakayama Shigeru to write this book, I accepted the task without hesitation. I first wrote two papers in English on this topic for two international conferences. This book was hastily written based on these two papers. As a result, I confess that the work has not rid itself of the academic tone and I regret that it does not make an easy read.

Whenever I look around in bookstores, I am surprised to see how books related to astrology have proliferated compared to the past. These are mostly things that confuse people, stir up their insecurities and take advantage of human weaknesses. While it is not my intention to confront and criticize popular astrology, I wish to show in this book that when astrology is examined historically, we cannot help but be critical.

I would like to thank Furuya Shōji of Tokyo Bijutsu, who read through the first draft from the beginning and made numerous comments and suggestions.

Michio Yano

Kyoto
November 1986

Bibliography

Japanese

Ishida Mikinosuke 石田幹之助 . 1967.『長安の春 東洋文庫』. 東京: 平凡社 .

——. 1973.『東亞文化史藪考』. 東京: 東洋文庫 . 東洋文庫論叢.

Itō Gikyō 伊藤義教 1980.『ペルシア文化渡来考』. 東京: 岩波書店 .

Momo Hiroyuki 桃裕行. 1975.「宿曜道と宿曜勘文」『立正史学』39:1–20.

——. 1978.「日延の符天暦齎来」『律令国家と貴族社会[正]』. 竹内理三博士還暦記念会（編）. 東京: 吉川弘文館.

Morita Ryūsen 森田竜僊. 1941.『密教占星法』. 高野山: 高野山大学出版部.

Nakayama Shigeru 中山茂 . 1972.『日本の天文学』. 東京: 岩波書店. 岩波新書 .

——. 1979.『占星術』. 東京: 紀伊国屋書店.

Nojiri Hōei 野尻抱影 . 1971.『星と東方美術』. 東京: 恒星社厚生閣.

Ōkubo Kenji 大久保健治. 1981.『密教占星法と源氏物語 : 源氏物語の見失われた構造』. 東京: 河出書房新社.

Watanabe Toshio 渡辺敏夫 . 1976.『日本の暦』. 東京: 雄山閣.

Yabuuti Kiyoshi 薮内清. 1944.『隋唐暦法史の研究 東方文化研究所東洋暦術調査事業報告』. 東京: 三省堂.

——. 1980.『歴史はいつ始まったか』. 中公新書.

——. 1982.「唐曹士蔿の符天暦について」.『ビアリア』78.

——. 1989.『隋唐暦法史の研究』. 増訂版 1944. 京都: 臨川書店.

——. 1990.「増補改訂中国の天文暦法」. 平凡社.

Yano Michio 矢野道雄. 1980.『インド天文学・数学集 科学の名著』. 東京: 朝日出版社.

——. 1992.『占星術師たちのインド』. 中公新書. 東京: 中央公論社.

——. 2004.『星占いの文化交流史』. シリーズ言葉と社会. 東京: 勁草書房.

——. 2011.『インド数学の発想 **IT** 大国の源流をたどる』. 東京: NHK 出版部 .

——. 2016.「『宿曜経』の大蔵経本と和本の比較〔改正版〕(A Comparison of Two Recensions of the *Xiuyao Jing* [Revision])」『日本古写経研究所研究紀要』1:1–11.

Yano Michio 矢野道雄 and Sugita Mizue 杉田瑞枝 1995.『占術大集成』. 東京: 平凡社.

Yano Michio 矢野道雄 and Hayashi Takao 林隆夫. 2013.「『宿曜経』の二系統と同志社写本」『密教占星術』（増補改訂）. 東京: 東洋書院 . L264–L251.

Yoshida Mitsukuni 吉田光邦. 1970.『星の宗教』. 京都: 淡交社.

Zenba Makoto 善波周. 1956.「仏典の天文暦法について」『印度学仏教学研究』4.1 (一月):18–27.

——. 1952.「摩登伽経の天文暦数について」『小西・高畠・前田三教授頌壽記念：東洋学論叢』. 京都: 平楽寺書店. 171–241.

Western

al-Bīrūnī. Sachau, Eduard (trans.). 1993. *Alberuni's India*. Frankfurt am Main: Institute for the History of Arabic-Islamic Science at the Johann Wolfgang Goethe University.

Bouché-Leclercq, Auguste. 1899. *Astrologie Grecque*. Paris: GDZ Sammlung Mathematica.

Goldstine, Herman H. 1973. *New and Full Moons 1001 BC to AD 1651*. Philadelphia: American Philosophical Society.

Ho Peng Yoke. 2003. *Chinese Mathematical Astrology: Reaching out to the Stars*. London; New York: Routledge Curzon.

Hunger, H. and R. Dvorak. 1981. *Ephemeriden von Sonne, Mond und hellen Planeten von 1000 bis 601*. Wien: Österreichischen Akademie der Wissenschaften.

Mak, Bill M. 2013a. "The date and nature of Sphujidhvaja's *Yavanajātaka* reconsidered in the light of some newly discovered materials." *History of Science in South Asia* 1:1–20.

——. 2013b. "The Last Chapter of Sphujidhvaja's *Yavanajātaka* critically edited with notes." *SCIAMVS* 14:59–148.

Manilius, Marcus and G.P. Goold. 1977. *Astronomica*. The Loeb Classical Library. Cambridge, Mass.; London: Harvard University Press; W. Heinemann.

Miyazaki, Tensho, Jundo Nagashima, Tatsushi Tamai and Liqun Zhou. 2015. "The Śārdūlakarṇāvadāna from Central Asia." In *The St. Petersburg Sanskrit Fragments*. Tokyo: Soka University. 1–84.

Nakayama Shigeru. 1969. *A History of Japanese Astronomy*. Cambridge, Mass.: Harvard University Press.

Neugebauer, O. and H.B. Van Hoesen. 1959. *Greek Horoscopes*. Philaedelphia, Pa.: American Philosophical Society.

Neugebauer, O. 1957. The Exact Sciences in Antiquity. 2nd ed. New York: Dover, 1969.

Pelliot, Paul and Éd. Chavannes. 1913. "Un traité manichéen retrouvé en Chine II." *Journal Asiatique* 1–11:99–199, 261–392.

Pingree, David Edwin. 1978. *The Yavanajataka of Sphujidhvaja*. Harvard Oriental Series Vol.48. Cambridge: Harvard University Press.

Pingree, David. 1981. *Jyotiḥśāstra: Astral and Mathematical Literature*. Wiesbaden: Harrassowitz.

Ptolemy. 1971. Edited and translated by F.E. Robbins. *Tetrabiblos*. London; Cambridge, MA: William Heinemann; Havard University Press.

Tuckerman, Bryant. 1962. *Planetary, Lunar, and Solar Positions 601 BC To AD 1 at Five-Day and Ten-Day Intervals*. Philadelphia: American Philosophical Society.

Yabuuti, Kiyosi. 1979. "Researches on the *Chiu-chih li*." *Acta Asiatica* 36:7–48.

Yano, Michio. 1986. "The *Ch'iyao jang-tsai-chueh* and its Ephemerides." Centaurus 29:28–35.

——. 1987. "The *Hsiu-yao Ching* and its Sanskrit Sources." In *History of Oriental Astronomy*. Cambridge: Cambridge University Press. 125–34.

——. 1990. "Ptolemy in China." In *Documents et Archives provenant de l'Asie Centrale*. Kyoto: Association Franco-Japonaise des Études Orientales. 217–20.

——. 1995. "A Planetary Ephemeris in Japanese Buddhist Astrology: A Case of Transmission." In *East Asian Science: Tradition and Beyond*. Osaka: Kansai University Press. 73–81.